# The self·ish SERVANT

## Inspirational Lessons from a Visionary CEO to Create Extra • Ordinary Life

ANTONIO MCBROOM

# ADVANCE PRAISE FOR ANTONIO MCBROOM AND THE SELF•ISH SERVANT

"McBroom's timeless principles of tenacity, self-awareness, passion and gratitude in *The Self•ish Servant* are ones I've leaned on personally and professionally as a *Fortune* 50 CEO. This book is an inspiration and a tactical resource for other leaders looking to create a 'CEO Life,' as McBroom creatively calls it."

—Marvin R. Ellison, Chairman, President and CEO Lowes Companies Inc., a *Fortune* 50 company in home improvement

"*The Self•ish Servant* blends a seamless narrative with lessons I've tried to apply in my own life over decades. From the entrepreneurial grit needed to create a thriving business to the humility needed to live a life of service, the stories McBroom shares add up to a book and a life that are truly distinguished."

—Barbara Hyde, CEO and Chair, Hyde Family Foundation

"After working with McBroom since the early days of Primo Partners, I've witnessed firsthand the results of his bravery, commitment to excellence and strategic risk-taking. It has led to the meteoric growth of both his companies and an ever-expanding personal impact on others. His life story in *The Self•ish Servant* is an example any aspiring entrepreneur can learn from—and he is just getting started."

—Jason Garey, All-American and Hermann Trophy Winner as Best College Soccer Player, Award Winning Wealth Management Advisor

ISBN: 978-1-964377-53-7 (ebook)

ISBN: 978-1-964377-52-0 (paperback)

ISBN: 978-1-964377-54-4 (hardcover)

ISBN: 978-1-964377-55-1 (audiobook)

For more information about Antonio McBroom and additional resources for *The Self•ish Servant,* scan the QR code below:

# CONTENTS

# PART I: CREATING

*Verb*:

Late Middle English (in the sense "form out of nothing," used of a divine or supernatural being): from Latin *creat-* 'produced', from the verb *creāre.*

Bring(ing) something into existence. To cause something to happen as a result of one's actions.

# CHAPTER 1
# TENACITY + PERSEVERANCE

## NOT LEVEL ONE, NOT LEVEL TWO, BUT LEVEL TEN-ACITY

*"The ultimate measure of a person is not where they stand in times of comfort and convenience, but where they stand at times of challenge and controversy."*
—Martin Luther King, Jr.

My mom was the first in our family to graduate from college, and she set the bar high. From a very young age, she taught me the three pillars of life: God, family and education. When I was one year old, my bio dad was incarcerated. This loss was the beginning of a life-long lesson about the value of family, a pillar we can't live without.

Mom was a teacher, and she relied on the help of her mother, my Memaw, to take care of me while she commuted to work at a school in Siler City, about 30 minutes away from our home in Goldson, North Carolina. Memaw's house was antiquated, but it was full of love. We had an outside johnny house with a red bucket for a toilet, and a wood-burning stove for our heat. There was no plumbing or running water, so one of my chores was to run over to the neighbor's house with a bucket, fill it with water from their tap, then haul it back home. We brushed our teeth with a mug and heated our baths on the stove. I didn't think this was out of the ordinary—it was all normal to us.

Memaw's home was the family's gathering spot, and there was always something on the stove to eat. She was also the first entrepreneur I knew. By day, her 1940s two-bedroom house was a daycare, with my cousins and me running in and out, screen door slamming nonstop. Her house was right next door to the town greasy spoon, so by night Memaw seized an opportunity: she made a little extra cash by turning her kitchen into a rural night club for locals, serving up the finest bootleg liquor.

Like most rural Southern towns, Goldston was poor and tough. But the love I got from Mom, Memaw, my family and church community filled in all the gaps and shaped me into the man I am.

When I was five, Mom started up a romance with an old high school love, Pruitt, and they decided to move us closer to Siler City so I could start first grade at her school. This move meant we were living a more traditional family life, and eventually we welcomed my little brother, PJ.

I thrived in elementary school, all due to Mom's watchful eye. I developed a passion for math, and even though I was young, I was well on my way to becoming a scholar athlete. Both physically and emotionally, I grew up fast. I was always the tallest person in school, and after an impressive growth spurt, I was six foot one in sixth grade. Known as "Little Shaq," I played AAU basketball and landed on the best team in the state.

Those early days as an athlete gave me my first taste of leadership: because I was the biggest guy on the team, I was team captain, and I rose to the challenges and responsibilities that came with the role. Playing on that team also gave me my first taste of my insatiable thirst for travel. Our trips to Florida, Tennessee and Myrtle Beach gave me an opportunity to see how other people lived, making the world a little less intimidating.

Riding the high of athletic and academic success, I wasn't prepared for the challenges waiting around the corner. My stepdad was a veteran who struggled with post-traumatic stress disorder, a condition that has affected many people who have served in active duty. PTSD used to be called "battle fatigue," and soldiers who suffered from it were often seen as weak or soft because they couldn't process the trauma they had experienced during war. Thank goodness, we've come a long way in our understanding of this condition. The mental, emotional and spiritual strains of combat are proof of our humanity.

These days, PTSD can be managed with access to the right support, but Pruitt was not so lucky. After witnessing the horrific death of a colleague and friend, he replayed the event over and over in his head, causing him to suffer from extreme anxiety and panic attacks. As a result, he—like so many—tried to soothe his PTSD symptoms with drugs and alcohol, eventually developing a dependency which put a strain on his relationships. Even though he usually took care of us and provided for our basic needs, his reasoning was clouded by his substance use, so he didn't always make the best decisions.

At the same time, our landlords were charged with tax fraud, and as a result we were evicted from our home. So we all moved back to Goldston, and because Pruitt and I weren't seeing eye to eye, I chose to go back and live with Memaw.

I am happy to report that with time, maturity and a deeper understanding of addiction and mental health, Pruitt and I have been able to heal those wounds and restore our relationship. Most importantly, Pruitt has been sober for over a decade. I hope anyone reading this who struggles with PTSD, addiction or other mental health challenges knows that there's help and there's hope: you aren't alone. Level TEN-acity and perseverance are both superpowers that will propel you in your struggle.

---

Memaw spoiled me with pancakes for breakfast, fried cornbread for lunch, fried chicken for dinner and Kool-Aid by the gallons—

so moving back in with her was the easiest part of this transitional time. Finding my way at a new school and as an older kid, however, presented another set of challenges. I didn't make the best choices when it came to picking friends, and as smart as I was academically, I was making plenty of dumb decisions: dabbling in local gang activity, not prioritizing school and living what I now call that "wanksta" life. Eventually, those bad decisions led to me getting kicked off the basketball team. And as terrible as that felt, the bottom really fell out when I was 13 and in eighth grade.

One day, Mom sat me down and told me she had been diagnosed with lupus, an auto-immune disease that severely impacts daily life. Her condition meant flare-ups that impacted her organ function and caused extreme joint pain, which kept her from working full-time. Her life as she knew it was about to change dramatically.

That conversation was a bucket of cold water thrown over my head, waking me up and reminding me of the values I was raised with. My steady, unshakeable mom had always been my support system through life's ups and downs. Now she was impacted by a disease outside her control, and she was a major example of perseverance and tenacity.

*"Do not judge me by my successes, judge me by how many times I fell down and got back up again."*
—Nelson Mandela

That talk with Mom was my first real life-coaching session. She told me that because of her diagnosis, she didn't know how long she'd be around to support me, or how much she'd be able to help me succeed. My future was in my hands, and if I wanted to make something of myself, it was up to me.

I had already observed how money could alter life experiences. If I had a few dollars in my pocket, I could treat myself to a McFlurry at McDonald's instead of just ordering from the dollar menu. Now I saw that if I wanted to access opportunities, I would have to make some money. Mom was no longer able to teach full time, so money was going to be even tighter at home. I had seen how Memaw's entrepreneurial thinking had kept a roof over our heads, so I started looking for possible ways to make money.

My first business was doing yard work around the neighborhood. I made a few dollars trimming grass, pulling weeds, shaping bushes and raking leaves. This was great for a while, but eventually my peers caught on to the idea and started competing with me. I had to find a way to corner a market that set me apart from the other kids.

I had always excelled at math, and in those last years of middle school and early high school, I realized that my friends' parents valued my skills and were willing to pay me to tutor their kids. Being rewarded for my strengths helped build my confidence, and I started high school with focus and determination.

When you're from a small county in the South, chances are you're related to almost everyone you meet. The folks working at the corner store are aunts or uncles, and the kids at school are first, second or third cousins. When I got to high school, I was no longer the tallest kid—my peers had caught up to me, removing that edge I had enjoyed while playing middle school basketball, so I started playing football. That was when I was lucky enough to connect with my cousin (or *primo*, as he'd be called in Spanish), Eric.

Eric was older than me, a senior when I was a freshman. He was straightlaced and clean-cut, an honor roll student taking all AP classes and Salutatorian for his graduating class. I saw the array the opportunities before him and I wanted them too. He became my mentor, and this was the beginning of a life-long relationship that has always been at the center of my success.

One of my first tough lessons in high school was that becoming a professional athlete wasn't a life plan for me. I had to shift my focus away from athletics and develop an impressive academic resume. Eric taught me what hard work and focus really look like. He inspired me to make my time in high school as impactful as possible, and to create my own opportunities.

Tenacity is the quality someone demonstrates through determination on their way to achieving a goal. It is more than stubbornness. It is a level of commitment combined with the required knowledge and skills to achieve victory. Tenacity is what drove me to become a leader on my high school campus. I became the BETA club president and the student body president. I joined the yearbook staff and learned about fund-raising. Eventually, I became the editor of the yearbook and learned about how to plan and accomplish a long-term project while leading others to accomplish small goals along the way.

Like many Southern schools, our high school was pretty segregated: the Black kids tended to stick with the Black kids, and the white kids with the white. This could be tough. Dating across race lines was pretty much impossible, and when you're basically related to every other Black kid at school, meeting new girls could be a real challenge. After a painful racial incident at our school that involved a noose and the NAACP, I saw the value of bridging the communication and racial gap. With the help of my mom and church elders, I started an on-campus organization that was focused on mending race relationships.

With Memaw, Mom, Eric and leaders in my church as examples of service to others, I was inspired to create the club we called SAVE: Students Actively Volunteering Everywhere. Our group was focused on helping the elderly—cleaning up their yards and spending time with them in nursing homes, playing games and socializing. The elders we partnered with imparted legacy life lessons, and some of them became my best friends.

During my senior year of high school, I was totally focused on the big picture of how I wanted to shape my future life. So when I was faced with the tough choice of attending basketball camp or Governor's School (what my teammates called "nerd camp"), I knew which option was going to lead me down the path of success.

Governor's School immersed me in a group of the nation's most academically-achieving kids. One year before heading off to college, I had the opportunity to live on a college campus and get a taste of dorm life and the academic rigors to come.

Having fully committed to approaching my future with tenacity, I worked closely with my guidance counselor, Ms. Andrews, to apply for scholarships and prepare for interviews. My grades were excellent and so were my SAT scores (I had nearly a perfect score in math). Colleges were reaching out to *me*, trying to recruit me. Scholarship opportunities were abundant, but once I was awarded the Morehead-Cain scholarship, the decision was easy.

The Morehead-Cain scholarship is the oldest and most prestigious full-merit undergraduate scholarship in the country, and it is a particularly big deal for a North Carolinian. This merit-based award program finds the best young leaders in the US and sends them to UNC Chapel Hill with a four-year, fully funded academic scholarship that covers tuition, room and board, books, a living stipend and even a laptop computer. There are summer enrichment opportunities that the rich and famous envy, including international research, outdoor leadership and world-class internships. Although I had choices like Yale and Duke on the table alongside my mom's HBCU alma mater NC A&T, the Morehead-Cain scholarship matched my passion for becoming a leader committed to community-building. The program provided a lifetime of networking opportunities, invested in my future and gave me the framework for creating an extraordinary life.

It's incredible for me now to look back at that conversation I had with my mom when I was 13. At such a young age, I had experienced what felt like a lot of loss: my birth dad, my family security, my stepdad and my mom's health and vitality. When she told me that it was up to me to make something of myself, that I could create my own choices and opportunities and that our family's legacy was on my shoulders, I can see now which value she was teaching me without even using the word: tenacity.

Years later, during my senior year of college, when I was facing some major life decisions about which professional path I would take, my *primo* Eric and I regrouped. That connection we formed in high school empowered us and fueled our drive for a life and success beyond our dreams. We weighed the risks and rewards of the myriad choices ahead of me. All my hard work, dedication, determination, focus and perseverance had led me to this pivotal moment, so it made perfect sense for both of us to take the *biggest risk*. We knew our tenacity would see us through, and together we formed our company, Primo Partners.

At the heart of our business is a set of values that act as our North Star: Servant Leadership, World-Class Hospitality and Growth. But we can't achieve any of these or inspire others to rise to the top without tenacity pumping through our veins. It is a permanent requirement for professional success and for CEO Life—Creating an Extra•Ordinary Life.

In the years since forming Primo, we've honed our definition of tenacity into bite-sized pieces, or what we call The Four Concepts of Tenacity. These concepts can guide you through any challenge, and help you reach your highest potential, success and fulfillment.

## CONCEPT ONE: REACH FOR ASPIRATIONS BUT SET ACHIEVABLE GOALS

Tenacity begins with differentiating between aspirations and goals. Aspirations require hope and ambition, and require us to dream bold dreams. Alternately, goals are more focused, and are achievable accomplishments that we strategically aim for.

Goals are stepping stones on the path to our aspirations. For example, at my company Primo, we have aspirations to leave a $10 billion legacy impact on business excellence by running a diverse and equitable company and sharing our vision with other leaders.

Our five-year goal, on the other hand, is to invest $10 million back into our community to enlighten our leaders so they can pay it forward. Here's another example: in my personal life, I aspire to share my message as a keynote speaker on all seven continents. As of the writing of this book, I've spoken in two, and have a goal to add a new continent within the next 12 months.

By setting the right goals at the right time while recruiting the right people and taking advantage of all of their resources, CEO-Lifers set their life stage for success. If your aspiration is the destination, goals are the vehicle to get you there and tenacity is the fuel that keeps you moving. You will find that your tenacity fuel tank is refilled with every achieved goal or accomplishment on your way to reaching your aspiration.

## CONCEPT TWO: PRACTICE DISCIPLINE IN *SERIAL TASKING*, NOT MULTITASKING

The human brain can process 11 million bits of information per second. That's a lot of thoughts! It makes sense that with so much processing power, we believe we can get a lot more accomplished if we're doing a bunch of different things at once. Taking a phone call while making dinner. Finishing a project while sitting in a meeting, while eating lunch, while texting your spouse about dinner plans, while checking the traffic to figure out how long it will take you to get home. How else will we get anything done?

In Chapter 7, I go deeper into the myth of multitasking, but the big takeaway is that researchers have determined that it is not an efficient strategy to accomplish anything meaningfully or effectively. Instead, it scatters focus in an already highly scattered brain and demands too much of our cognitive skills.

On the other hand, *serial tasking*—prioritizing, focusing and executing—is a much more effective approach to accomplishing tasks. Once you learn to resist the distractions that scatter your focused attention, you'll find your quality of work improves.

If you think about it, when we multitask it's usually because we feel overwhelmed by all the things we need to get finished, so we try to do everything at once. But if we instead *organize* our tasks by *prioritizing, focusing and executing,* we bring meaningful attention and intention fueled by tenacity to each task, and we feel that rush of accomplishment from a job well done.

When we want to CEO Life, we need tenacity, and we fuel the capacity for tenacity as we see task after task being successfully accomplished.

## CONCEPT THREE: LEARN HOW TO INITIATE AND MAINTAIN SMALL CHANGES AS THE FOUNDATION FOR LARGER CHANGES

Making highly desired change happen is difficult. The larger the change, the tougher the challenge. One way to make change more manageable is to divide it into smaller parts. By focusing on smaller adjustments, any mistakes that come up are not nearly as devastating. And when those missteps happen, we learn from them and incorporate the lessons for a better outcome next time.

Small changes build upon each other and become the foundation from which we can obtain the larger changes down the line. Think of an enormous domino setup. Highly skilled, creative people imagine a big picture, say a city skyline, and they go about setting up domino after domino in rows and sections to construct that elaborate scene. The only way the big reveal will succeed is if every little domino is set up perfectly. Do mistakes happen? I'd be willing to bet that on the way to creating a domino masterpiece, plenty of dominos are accidentally tipped over, creating a—you guessed it—domino effect of mistakes. Over time, the creators will learn that if they focus on small sections of the bigger picture, leaving a few empty spots to stop a chain-reaction disaster, their final reveal will be a brilliant success.

When Eric and I first formed Primo, we could more or less read each other's minds. We had the same work ethic and value system, so we didn't even have to talk about it. But as our business began to grow and we brought in more staff and team members, we learned that to maintain our business ethos, we had to define it. To build a company with the spirit of tenacity and the values of servant leadership, world-class hospitality and growth, we have to curate and cultivate every new hire. For each new team member, we craft an extraordinary integration experience. We invite all new employees to our headquarters for a personal introduction to our company culture. Living, breathing examples of Southern hospitality, we pick our guests up at the airport and bring them to the best local coffee shops.

The domino effect of this treatment is that those managers then follow our example and project warmth and hospitality to each of their new ice cream franchise scoopers. When a new employee shows up at the store for their first day on the job, their name tag is ready, the store is set up, the music is going and the waffle cone smell is in the air. Because they feel valued, they protect our company environment and project our core values.

Over time, we developed the proprietary Primo Kulture Lab™, a training and leadership development program that clearly breaks down our culture in small, digestible bites of performance expectations. Each small change our team members make in their mentality and behavior contributes to the whole picture, shifting everything they thought they knew about being an employee. As we've learned, this development program has a lasting, big-picture impact on our customers, our business and our communities.

The Primo Kulture Lab™ dynamically explains our values: servant leadership, world-class hospitality and growth. It also sets out the behaviors we expect to see that make Primo special. As each team member learns to center these values and behaviors in all that they do, they fuel our growth as a company. They become tenacious ambassadors for Primo. The daily behaviors and fundamentals below allow us to live our aspirational core values.

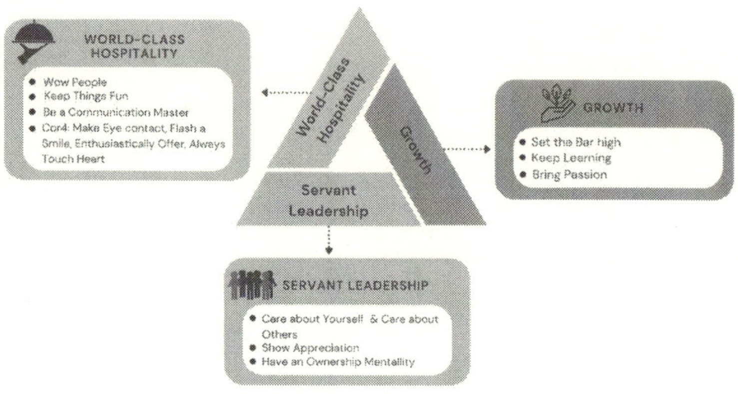


## CONCEPT FOUR: BUILD SKILLS FOR NAVIGATING ALL TYPES OF WINDS—HEADWINDS, TAILWINDS AND WHIRLWINDS

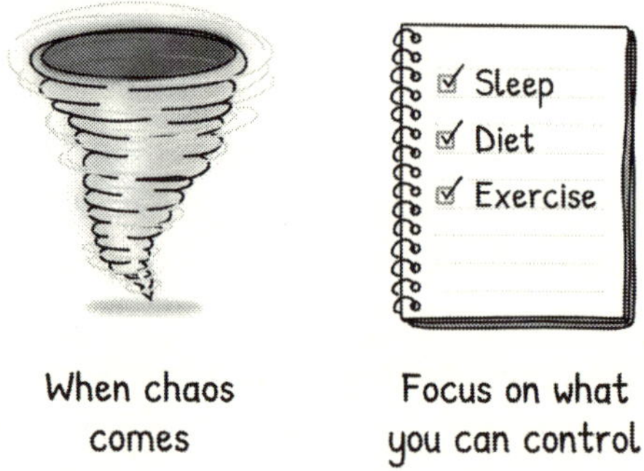


Agility is an important feature of TEN-acity. Being able to anticipate, prepare and act with integrity in a diversity of environments enables extraordinary people to maintain a high state of readiness.

Recognize that progress rarely moves exactly as you may have originally planned. A prepared leader has Plans A, B and C to accommodate any type of scenario, expected or not. It's easier to face a challenge when you are ready and prepared to pivot if needed. NFL teams have playbooks with audibles to ensure a range of options for a quick change in a play, improving their team's chance of carrying the ball over the line.

Preparation means investigating and anticipating every potential outcome or challenge ahead of the finish line. You can have all the ambition in the world, but if you aren't prepared to handle what comes at you, the next surprise is going to trip you up and bring progress to a halt. The types of challenges you may encounter are what I call headwinds, tailwinds and whirlwinds.

## HEADWINDS

Forces that are outside your control are headwinds. They're the hurdles and obstacles that seemingly come out of nowhere, impeding or halting your progress. But just like having a weather report helps you prepare your outfit for the day, you can be aware of where the headwinds are coming from and get ready for their arrival. Proper awareness of impending headwinds helps you navigate your future.

In my personal life, having an incarcerated father and a mother with an auto-immune disease were headwinds—factors that were working against me from the outset. During Covid, massive change hit almost every company in the world—from major white-collar corporations to factory jobs. Supply chains shut down and offices were closed, forcing employees to work remotely.

Over time, there were signs that employees were in many ways experiencing a more balanced life, without long commutes and other on-site pressures. With a good bird's-eye view of these changes, some company leaders could make out the first signs of the "great resignation," a major headwind for our society and economy. By carefully monitoring employee satisfaction, those companies learned to operate differently, accommodating their workers' desires while maintaining productivity.

## TAILWINDS

Any time you have an advantage that propels you ahead, you have a tailwind. People born into wealth have advantages that someone raised in poverty will not experience.

Memaw's house didn't have running water, but Mom was a teacher who prepared me academically for an advanced middle school education, which then meant I had the tailwind of readiness for demanding classes in high school. Being in upper-level classes in high school gave me the tailwind of being in classrooms with older students, which in turn led to mentorship relationships and respect. Just like knowing your headwinds can help you prepare for challenges, knowing your tailwinds can prepare you for opportunities.

## WHIRLWINDS

Life happens in whirlwinds. My wife Katie and I started building our family right after college graduation, and our daughter Nia was born a year after we bought our first Ben & Jerry's franchise. Having a child, a new business and starting life as an adult all at the same time was a whirlwind! But no life fully lived is without its whirlwinds.

Occasional distractions from the goals you're trying to accomplish are normal parts of life. If you have kids, maybe it's their sports schedule. If you have a sick relative, maybe it's doctor's appointments. These are just facts of life—but how can you navigate these whirlwinds so that you're still able to keep some focus?

Even something as small as a last-minute meeting cancellation, a car accident or a rain storm can create a whirlwind in life.

Everyday incidents can create chaos in our planning and progress towards our goals. When you feel the spinning winds starting to circle you, maintain your accountability, your focus and your tenacity to keep moving forward. Small progress is still progress.

## THERE'S FORTUNE IN THE FOLLOW THROUGH

Tenacity cannot replace solid systems and standard operating procedures. To successfully CEO Life, make sure your policies reflect your values, that they're effectively communicated and that they are totally operational.

The concept of "grinding" in life demoralizes the servant leader, making it easy to reinforce outdated ideas of growth. In order to prepare yourself for success, focus on these three key priorities:

### 1. VALUES & DREAMS:

Focus on the fundamentals of your core values. What are the associated behaviors that reinforce your values? Maybe use your name, and write down what comes to you. (Example: JAMES: Joy, Agility, Meditative, Energetic, Servant.) Now recall the section on aspirations and goals: identify three major life aspirations you have as they relate to your Fitness, Finances, Family & Friends and Faith.

### 2. THE HEADWINDS & TAILWINDS FORCE FIELD:

Identify three to five headwinds that are resisting your aspirations. How heavy is the resistance on a scale of one to five? Now identify three to five tailwinds and rate them on the same scale, based on how much they are propelling you forward.

## 3. THE ONE THING

What is the ***one thing*** that, if done with Level TEN-acity, will propel you towards your dreams while staying true to your values, leveraging your tailwinds and mitigating those headwinds? Maybe it's ensuring that your administrative work, such as scheduling and bill paying, is up to your impeccable standards.

Alternatively, that *one thing* could also be to provide your inner circle of family, friends, and community with the agency they need to support your growth with consistent reinforcement and confidence. Or, that *one thing* could be doing *less* to accomplish more. Less multitasking. Less distraction. By identifying this *one thing*, it becomes a priority that will feed your tenacity and preparedness, fueling your ongoing success.

# CHAPTER 2
# SELF AWARENESS + PERSONAL GROWTH

## BECOMING SELF•ISH: OUTWARD BOUND, INWARD BOUND + COLLEGE BOUND

*"Self-love, self-awareness, self-regard all have one thing in common: they start with 'self'."*
—Antonio McBroom

I'm a lifelong student of leadership. It's fascinating to me. Family leadership, business leadership, tribal leadership, government leadership, community leadership, sports leadership—you name it, I love it.

There are leaders who delegate and have a hands-off approach, expecting workers to solve their own problems. Some leaders go military-style and are more authoritarian—they don't look for feedback or opinions and simply want their expectations met without excuses. There are transactional leaders, who use rewards and punishment to motivate their team and value discipline above everything else.

Democratic leadership expects participation from all involved with a commitment to the overall good: these leaders have the final say, but team members feel included and involved. Coaching leadership is all about developing team members to get the best performance out of everyone; it is positive and nurturing, with constant feedback.

Of all the leadership styles out there, only one encompasses my values and trumps them all, and that's the practice of servant leadership. Servant leadership is about making sure others' highest-priority needs are being met first. A servant leader focuses on the growth and well-being of the people and community they serve. Servant leadership advises that if serving is beneath you, then leadership is beyond you. The best leaders desire to serve others.

At my company Primo, one question we always ask in interviews is, "If you could have dinner with someone, dead or alive, who would it be and why?" I love hearing the answers and learn so much about people through these questions. For me, the answer is Dr. Martin Luther King Jr.

I was blessed to be raised by amazing, beautiful and strong Black women. In addition to instilling faith and work ethic in me, they also ensured that I knew the history of where I came from. My mom taught me all about Kwanzaa at a young age, and Dr. King Day was really the jumpstart of Black History Month in our household. It was a time when we'd fully immerse ourselves into the journey, history and trajectory of the Black race. Later, I went on to double major in African-American Studies and Mathematics at UNC, doing my best to be a sponge for great Black thought leaders such as Booker T. Washington and George Washington Carver—though to me, none were greater than the Reverend Dr. Martin Luther King Jr.

Dr. King was a very special brother—a one-of-one. His message of taking the higher moral road with nonviolent resistance, leading and mobilizing during an era of oppression and suppression literally changed all of our lives today—whatever your race, culture or background.

From the time I was 10 years old, I've had a poster of one of his quotes hanging on my wall, and this message is part of my very DNA—in fact, it's so important, I'm repeating it. You'll remember seeing it back in Chapter 1:

*"The true measure of a man is not where he stands at times of comfort and convenience, but where he stands in times of challenge and controversy."*

As much as perseverance and grit mean to me—they are my key strengths and superpowers—I believe it's not how good you *are* that matters, but how good you *want to be,* and the true measure of Dr. King's legacy for me is his living example of servant leadership.

I was raised by servants. My mom and grandmother lived in service of others and to God. Like Dr. King, they understood and taught me that to truly live the teaching of Christ, we must prioritize the needs of others over our own. I cannot be truly happy or successful if those around me are not happy and successful. This humility is at the heart of Christ's teachings, and Memaw and Mom lived it.

The church was the center of our lives when I was growing up, and that's where I built a strong foundation of faith that kept me stable and grounded all through my school years and now as a business owner, leader, husband and father. Every opportunity I had in athletics and school were a result of my mom and Memaw being of service to my success. I always knew that wherever I went in life, it was due to their support and my connection to my church community. But even with all that backing, it wasn't until 2004 that I learned first-hand the importance of being a self•*ish* servant leader. At the time, I was 17 years old and college-bound.

The summer before freshman year, my fellow scholarship winners and I participated in an outdoor leadership program that helped prepare us for the challenges we all faced in the coming years. This month-long program is successful because it strips young people of their comforts, forces them to stretch their limits and demands that they develop and discover new ways to grow.

The experience is arranged in partnership with Outward

Bound and immerses young people from all walks of life in the remote wilderness, where they learn to become responsible, how to balance risk and reward, and how to work and succeed as a team while remaining compassionate and bold—all while forming deep connections with people who have a totally different background than their own.

It was not my idea of a good time. I left my girlfriend back home in rural North Carolina and headed to remote Butte, Montana to camp and backpack 150 miles over the course of a month with a group of strangers made up of outdoor enthusiasts, juvenile delinquents (forced to be there for rehabilitation) and book-smart college kids like me. I had never slept outside before. To say I was a fish out of water is an understatement; I was on an alien planet in a different universe.

We hiked 11 to 12 miles each day, up and downhill with all our supplies carried on our backs. I ate dried fruit for meals. My only comfort was the contraband wet wipes that I had somehow smuggled in. We were surrounded by wild animals—including bears—and had to hang our packs in trees overnight so animals didn't attack us. I stayed afraid.

Our mission was to learn how to work as a group with people who were nothing like us, and we had to achieve a goal by a specific deadline. In our case, it was to backpack 150 miles over the next month to reach our pick up point. I now look back and realize that this was an important lesson in servant leadership: when you're an equal part of a group, you have to put everyone's strengths and needs on the table, and they all have equal weight. Some people are stronger and can carry more, some are more athletic and can move quickly, some have more experience in nature and can navigate—with or without a compass. Some can fish, some can hunt and some can build a fire. When you are contributing your strength or skill, you're serving the others while also leading.

On this expedition, I noticed that I got to disappear—it was my first real reset (I would later seek out reset opportunities throughout my professional career, even providing them for the people in my inner circle). I was far away from the expectations and distractions of my regular life, and the trip forced me to get some perspective. In the wilderness, I wasn't a scholar or a star athlete. I was a guy with a backpack and a member of a group, each of us with our own individual strengths and stretches, and we had no choice but to depend on each other.

The biggest and most memorable challenge that came with the Outward Bound experience was a three-day solo trip. Relying only on myself, I had to navigate from point A to point B, and most importantly, I had to stay alive. Did I mention that there were bears? I don't know if there's any better way in life to be truly alone. In the solitude of the wilderness, the noises in your head get louder—and so do your fears. I had to rely on myself and what's more, I had to face myself. But in that solitude, I became myself.

I remembered Bible verses that spoke of Jesus choosing solitude. In Matthew 6:6, Jesus instructs people to pray alone: "When you pray, go into your room, close the door and pray to your Father, who is unseen. Then your Father, who sees what is done in secret, will reward you." In the book of Luke, 5:16, it's written that Jesus would "withdraw to desolate places and pray." Mark 6:31-32 tells how Jesus told others to come with him to a quiet place to rest, away from the crowds. In my wildest imagination, I couldn't think of anywhere more "alone" than in those woods under that Big Sky. I felt close to God.

To occupy my mind and time, I focused on my passions, one of which was music. I sang to myself—some hymns and songs I could remember from church, which summoned my faith, and some hip hop classics that my teammates and I would use to hype us up before games like Jay-Z's "Hard Knock Life" or Biggie Smalls' "Juicy." I wrote a lot of letters to people, and some were apologies. I wrote vision letters, with my goals and dreams sketched out. I wrote letters to my future self to be opened on a specific date, years down the line. I was also learning about how to support my mental health, and one tool I used was a new routine I had learned from the Outward Bound leaders, the SAVERS, AKA the "Miracle Morning Routine." This ritual, similar to brushing my teeth, still helps me show up at my freshest each day as CEO of a growing business and dynamic life:

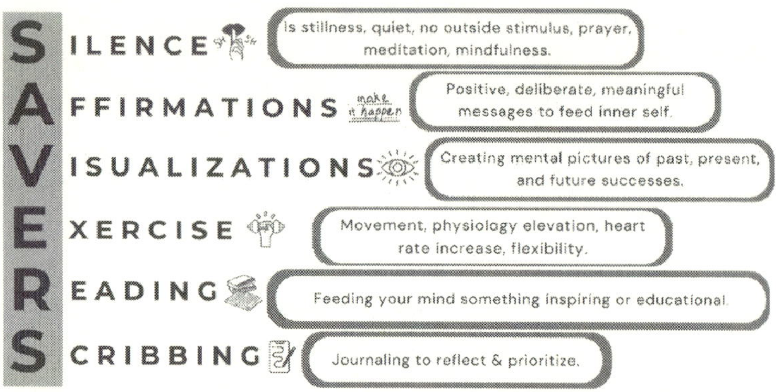


But the most powerful lesson I learned on that solo journey was how to be self•*ish*. This definition of "selfish" has nothing to do with when I indulge in all the chocolate chunks from a pint of Ben & Jerry's, leaving just the ice cream for my wife and kids. That kind of selfish we all learn when we're toddlers, when our most powerful vocabulary word is "mine."

I mean self•*ish*. You've been on the plane when the flight attendant announces the safety instructions in case of an emergency. They tell you to always put the oxygen mask on yourself before trying to help someone else. Just like you can't assist someone else when you can't breathe, you can't be of service if you haven't strengthened, cultivated and turned a microscopic focus on every part of your *self*.

But let's also look at the suffix "•*ish*." We use it to communicate *somewhat* or *approximately*. I'm thinking of the great TV show created by Kenya Barris, *Black•ish*. This program is hilarious and heartfelt, telling stories about straddling the lines between race and class in an affluent, mostly white community. The main character (played by Anthony Anderson) walks through the specific challenges that most successful, Black executives encounter in an almost exclusively white corporate world. He is challenged to hold on to his ethnic identity while raising kids who feel connected to their Black culture and comfortable in a world that demands assimilation. His wife is played by the legendary Tracee Ellis Ross, and we see her experiences of being mixed race and how she navigates between two races and cultures. We also get the flavor of three generations facing similar challenges in their own distinct ways. This show explores all the •*ish*es that come with identity. Old•*ish,* young•*ish,* rich•*ish,* got-it-all-together•*ish.*

We use this suffix all the time:

*"The sales person was thirty-ish."*
*"I'm meeting my date at five-ish."*

Someone might speak or be Dan*ish* or Span*ish*. Someone who reads a lot is book*ish*. I've even heard the suffix "-ish" used as a whole sentence!

*"Did you have a good day?"*
*"…-ish."*

"•*ish*" puts the emphasis on the "kind of" part of the word. Being self•*ish* doesn't mean self-obsessed or lacking regard for others as we have come to think of it. It's a new, contemporary spin on an old idea. Being self•*ish* simply means focusing on the "self" part in order to become better versions of ourselves. Being a self•*ish* servant isn't really about being selfish, it's only kind of about that—because when you add that "servant" at the end, you're clarifying that it's really about aiding others.

Other words go through definition changes over time as

contemporary usage evolves. The word "disrupt" technically means causing a disturbance or a problem. But Martin Luther King Jr. disrupted the racist status quo in the Jim Crow South, and eventually in our national laws. Henry Ford disrupted industrialization in his time by inventing the assembly line. Spotify disrupted the music industry by making *any and all* music streaming accessible from a hand-held device. Before that, digital file sharing disrupted how the entire music industry worked, eventually recreating how consumers got music. Love him or hate him, Elon Musk disrupted how cars are manufactured, bought and sold. These days in corporate and marketing circles, when someone "disrupts" something, it's ingenious. It's a new way of doing something that challenges the establishment or status quo.

Another example of how the meanings of words change is the word "collaborator." Back during World War II, being a collaborator was the worst thing you could be accused of. The phrase "loose lips sink ships" was on posters all over the county warning people about the dangers of revealing classified information or valuable intel that could embolden our enemies. But if you look at the word now, it's fundamental in successful business-building! Collaborating with others means that every person is contributing their skills, strengths and knowledge to help develop the whole.

My month in the wilderness under the big sky of Montana *disrupted* my comfortable life as a beloved (okay, spoiled) son and grandson and award-winning scholar. It taught me that if I can't rely on myself, I can't contribute to the overall success of the group—AKA, *collaborate*—and I can't be of any help to others. The broader application of this in the real world is that if I don't have a strong sense of self, I am foundationless, and nothing can be built without a foundation. If I want to build a life I'm proud of—a business, a family, a community or a world —I need to be a servant to others, and to do this, I must have an unshakable foundation of self.

In general, every type of self-development starts with self-reflection: focused thinking about your own character, your actions and your motives. This can be uncomfortable if you're not used to sitting quietly, diving deep into your emotions and examining yourself in the mental mirror. But it's important to look at your past and all the actions and decisions that led you to this moment, and to think about how your actions today contribute to who you will become tomorrow. Self-reflection is a requirement for becoming an extraordinary servant leader.

## Tools for Self-Reflection

Using these tools, here are some areas of focus and ways you can discover and develop your *self* on your way to becoming a self•*ish* servant:

## Valuing Yourself

| | WHAT IT MEANS | HOW TO DEVELOP |
|---|---|---|
| 01 Self-Love | Appreciating your own worth and value. Having compassion and willingness to unconditionally accept and celebrate who you are today. | Set boundaries to protect yourself emotionally; listen to your gut feelings and prioritize them; use positive affirmations; identify what you like and love, prioritize those things; spend time with yourself in solitude and develop a sense of connectedness to yourself and the world around you. |
| 02 Self-Worth | How you value your abilities, skills, strengths and contributions to a group or the world. | Make a list of your attributes as if you were talking about a friend; identify your strengths, and decide how you can use them to contribute to the overall good; notice when you're being unkind to yourself and turn it into something positive. |
| 03 Self-Awareness | Knowing your personal values and standards, you have a willingness to evaluate your thoughts, feelings and actions to discern whether they meet your—and others'—expectations. | Begin a meditation practice; explore therapy; seek feedback and accept criticism without becoming defensive; be grateful for all that you have; practice daily reflection by journaling. |
| 04 Self-Acceptance | Embracing every part of yourself and being comfortable with your positive, negative and in-progress attributes. | Learn to forgive yourself for mistakes or failings; when you set goals, make sure they're realistic; don't compare yourself to others; practice self care. |

## Growing Yourself

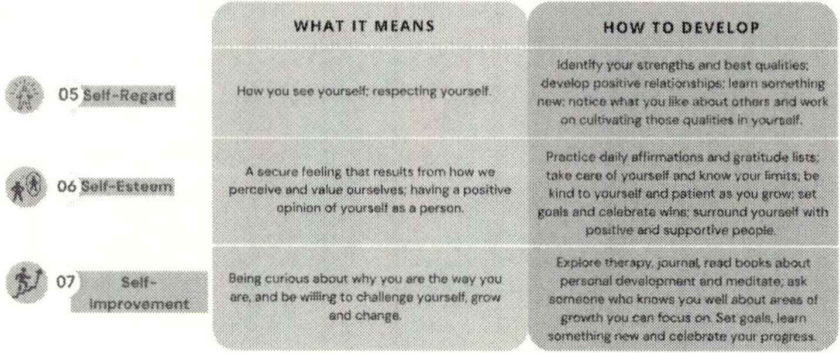

| | WHAT IT MEANS | HOW TO DEVELOP |
|---|---|---|
| 05 Self-Regard | How you see yourself; respecting yourself. | Identify your strengths and best qualities; develop positive relationships; learn something new; notice what you like about others and work on cultivating those qualities in yourself. |
| 06 Self-Esteem | A secure feeling that results from how we perceive and value ourselves; having a positive opinion of yourself as a person. | Practice daily affirmations and gratitude lists; take care of yourself and know your limits; be kind to yourself and patient as you grow; set goals and celebrate wins; surround yourself with positive and supportive people. |
| 07 Self-Improvement | Being curious about why you are the way you are, and be willing to challenge yourself, grow and change. | Explore therapy, journal, read books about personal development and meditate; ask someone who knows you well about areas of growth you can focus on. Set goals, learn something new and celebrate your progress. |

## Affirming Yourself

| | WHAT IT MEANS | HOW TO DEVELOP |
|---|---|---|
| 08 Self-Confidence | Having a positive attitude about and belief in yourself and your abilities. | Stand up for yourself, set goals with measurable results; dress well and practice healthy grooming habits; meditate; take care of your body and build physical strength. Don't compare yourself to others and practice positive self-talk; use daily affirmations. |
| 09 Self-Reliance | Unwavering trust in yourself and your ability to see your way through any challenge. | Challenge yourself and push outside your comfort zones. Believe you can do hard things, be disciplined and be patient with yourself as you learn and grow. |
| 10 Self-Sufficiency | Independence and strong autonomy; can take care of yourself in any situation. | Provide for yourself, pay your bills on time, grow your own food, cook for yourself; learn to trust yourself and your instincts. |

## WHAT IS A SELF•*ISH* SERVANT?

The self•*ish* servant is a leader who understands themselves so well that they can readily and effectively focus on developing and fortifying other people, their business, their community and the world. When you combine self•*ish* with service, you get a strong leader with main character energy.

Think of the main characters in your favorite movies. Typically, they are confident, charismatic and self-assured. They are in control of the narrative and drive the story forward. They go on a journey, face the monster and solve the problem or save the world. As you develop your *self,* you are making yourself the main character so that you embody those qualities of confidence. Only then can you lead others to success. I often tell my team we spend so much time on self-awareness and self-development because we deserve to work with the best versions of each other.

When you have that self•*ish* foundation, you can become a leader who focuses on the needs of others before your own—a servant leader. The servant leader philosophy is different from the typical top-down leadership most companies and organizations rely on.

Servant leaders are focused on their team members—their fulfillment, growth and happiness. Instead of authoritarian and control-focused leadership, the servant leader emboldens and cultivates the development of others so the power is shared and all contributors reach their highest potential.

The concept of servant leadership is as old as the Bible. Jesus was the ultimate servant leader, but the phrase itself was coined in 1970 by Robert K. Greenleaf in his essay *The Servant as Leader*. In it he wrote:

> The servant-leader is servant first…It begins with the natural feeling that one wants to serve, to serve first. Then conscious choice brings one to aspire to lead…Do those served grow as persons? Do they, while being served, become healthier, wiser, freer, more autonomous, more likely themselves to become servants?

"Healthy, wise, free and autonomous" are all qualities that result from being self•*ish* and focused on self-development. When you embody those qualities yourself, you can help cultivate them in others. ***There's no greater legacy we can leave than one of servant leadership!***

When I formed Primo with my cousin Eric, I had just graduated from college. At 21, I became the youngest franchise operator in Ben & Jerry's company history. Our company name was a double entendre: since Eric and I were cousins, Primo made sense because it is Spanish for "cousin." But in Black culture, "primo" means top shelf, the crème de la crème. We saw ourselves as top-shelf leaders, and the company we were starting was going to be a reflection of our passion, servant leadership and world-class hospitality all infused with the spirit of fun. We were starting with one franchise, but we knew that as we grew and hit our goals, we wouldn't stray from these values and we promised to deliver the "Ritz-Carlton and Disney experience in two scoops."

As we scaled our business, we learned that to really honor our value of servant leadership, we had to focus on leadership development. We came up with a collection of self-development concepts that can help any potential leader to CEO Life (Create an Extra•Ordinary Life).

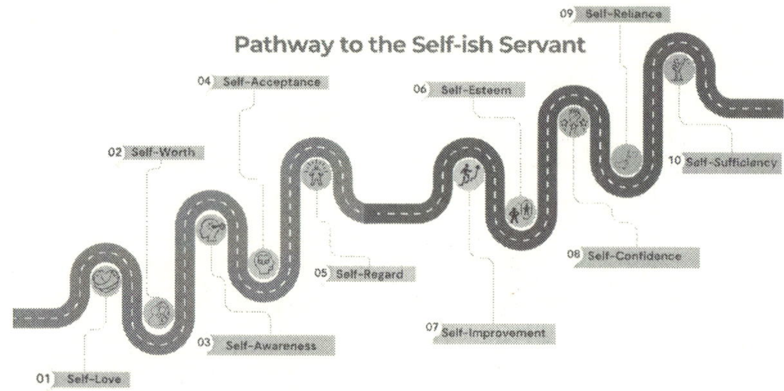

## THE FIVE CONCEPTS OF BECOMING A SELF•*ISH* SERVANT LEADER

### CONCEPT ONE: SELF-LEADERSHIP

You are always the leader of at least one person: yourself. You lead yourself through every day, week and month. As an effective leader, you must have deep knowledge of yourself as well as the people you lead. You must center self-leadership in your commitment to stretch, learn and grow—this enables you to be prepared and confident to meet every moment and opportunity.

How well do you know yourself? Who do you want to be? Write a list of words that describe the best version of yourself. How close are you to embodying each of these attributes? Commit to start, or keep doing the things that best demonstrate your self-leadership.

### CONCEPT TWO: SELF-MANAGEMENT IS NON-NEGOTIABLE

To CEO Life, you must be excellent at self-management. This means you have cultivated self-awareness to the extent that you have the agility and ability to manage your own actions, interactions, reactions and emotions. It is nearly impossible to create a respectful, high-performing culture for your business if it's being led by someone who is not self-managed. Take yourself on as your first project.

There are five key "Cs" to self-awareness: Character, Competence, Capacity, Consistency and Confidence. Reflect on each of these characteristics and rate yourself; note where you are meeting your own high standards and where there is room for improvement. Become intentional about maintaining or exceeding your high ratings while improving your ratings in other areas.

## CONCEPT THREE: SELF-LOVE IS NOT NARCISSISM—IT IS A NECESSITY

Self-love is defined as "high regard for one's own well-being and happiness." Self-love is about taking responsibility for your own needs and not denying those needs to please other people. Leaders who cannot or will not practice self-love are significantly challenged to express love, concern and respect for others. It all starts with *you*!

In his article "Six Differences Between Narcissism and Self-Love," Fahim Chughtai explains how we can tell these two apart. Narcissism is self-centeredness and a sense of entitlement that lacks empathy. A narcissist manipulates others to control them and their behavior and has an extreme need for attention: it's quite often a personality disorder that cannot be treated with traditional talk therapy. Self-love is a state of mind. It's the radical acceptance of yourself as you are, without judgment or conditions.

Here are the six differences between narcissism and self-love, according to Chughtai:

1. Narcissism is about being in love with oneself; self-love is simply accepting and loving oneself.
2. Narcissism is a disorder that requires help from a professional; self-love is a completely natural and healthy state of being.
3. People with narcissism often have low self-esteem; people with self-love generally have high self-esteem.
4. Narcissists are often critical of others; those with self-love accept others and themselves for who they are.
5. Narcissists need a lot of admiration and attention from others; those who love themselves don't need validation from anyone else.
6. Narcissism is often harmful to both the individual and to relationships; self-love is always beneficial to both the individual and to relationships.

## CONCEPT FOUR: SELF-EXAMINATION TEACHES LEADERS TO HONESTLY ASSESS THEIR OWN ABILITIES AND THE ABILITIES OF OTHERS

Understanding and acknowledging your own talent is the basis of learning how to affirm and trust the talents of others. Leaders who have taken the time to be confident in their own capabilities are much better at bringing out the best in those they lead. When a leader is confident, it is easier to share power and responsibilities across the team. Remember: with servant leadership, the group shares the power. Practicing and encouraging self-examination creates an environment where constructive feedback is embraced as a part of the collective learning journey.

## CONCEPT FIVE: SELF-RELIANCE ENABLES LEADERS TO BUILD AGILITY AND RESILIENCE

Some of life's most important and lasting lessons are learned through discomfort. When challenged physically, mentally or emotionally, leaders learn what they can achieve under pressure and in times of uncertainty. Leaders need these challenging learning experiences combined with more traditional training methods to be at a heightened state of readiness for the continuously unpredictable world of business.

## THERE'S FORTUNE IN THE FOLLOW THROUGH

It's time to build your own understanding of yourself. That foundation is fundamental to fortifying other people, supporting their goals, developing your community and changing the world. When you combine self•*ish* with service, you become that main character energy.

1. Take a moment and be self•*ish*. Close your eyes and visualize three things that you want. I don't mean "today items," I mean big-picture, transformational

upgrades for yourself. It can be characteristics you want to develop, things you want to achieve, or the impact you want to leave behind. Expand your self-identity right now and project it into the future. What is your legacy?

2. Look at the Five Cs to Self Awareness: Character, Competence, Capacity, Consistency and Confidence. Reflect on each of these and rate yourself; note where you are meeting your own high standards and where there is room for improvement. These Five Cs will guide you toward realizing the new vision of self that you have envisioned.

**Characteristics of the Effective Leader**

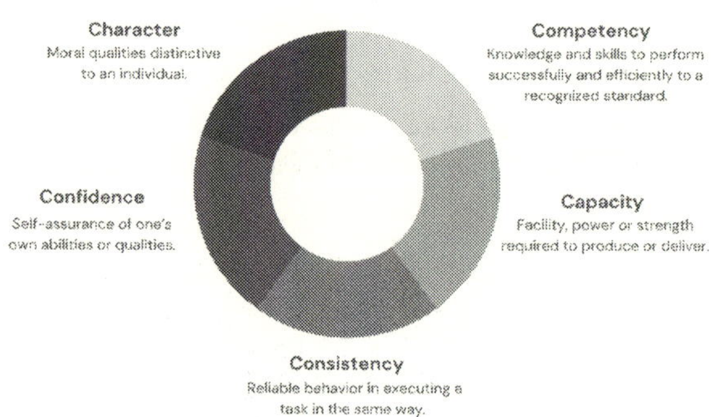


3. What is the one thing you can do today to become more self•*ish*? How about this week? Of the five areas of focus towards becoming self•*ish*, what is the *one* that will have the biggest impact on your journey to CEO Life?

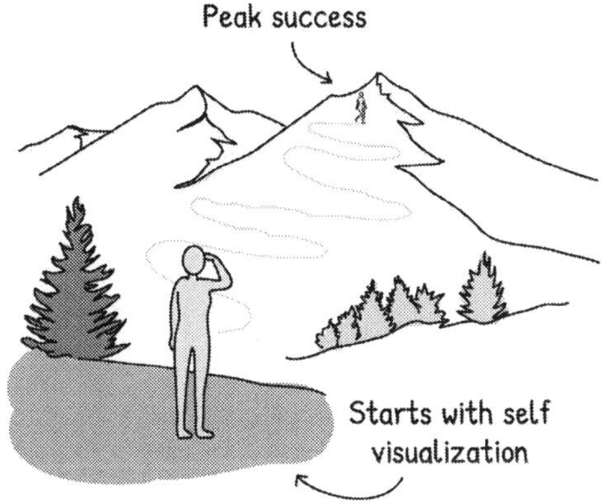
Peak success
Starts with self visualization
@Quoted Visually

# CHAPTER 3
# PASSION + AND

## THE LONG WALK FROM SOUTH AFRICA TO ATLANTA

*"The test of first-rate intelligence is the ability to hold two opposing ideas in the mind at the same time and still retain the ability to function."*
—F. Scott Fitzgerald

Being a Morehead-Cain scholar meant opportunities. The first summer break after my freshman year was known as the "Service Summer," and the world became my campus. In 2005, I was asked where in the world I would like to travel. Through the WorldTeach organization, I would be set up with a host family and teaching job in a totally foreign culture and environment. Talk about boundary-stretching!

I had recently read Nelson Mandela's *A Long Walk to Freedom,* and I was inspired by Mandela's passion for the topics of racial reconciliation and forgiveness, and the parallels he drew between Apartheid in South Africa and the Jim Crow South in America. I was passionate about empowering my community and honoring my culture, and I wanted to see first-hand how Black and brown societies were living out the ramifications of oppression just ten years after Apartheid, as well as how their experiences mirrored those in my own country. So I chose Cape Town, South Africa.

## FROM SOUTH AFRICA...

This was my first time getting a passport, my first trip out of the country and my first time seeing life outside of North Carolina. Sure, I had been to Montana for my Outward Bound experience, but the mountains of the Big Sky state were a far cry from an international flight and the sounds of new languages and accents spoken around me every day. My cohorts on the trip were mostly Ivy Leaguers from Harvard, MIT and Berkeley. I didn't naturally connect with them because our life experiences were so different. However, once you're outside the familiarity and comforts of your own country, having compatriots can really help you feel closer to home.

It was a strange feeling landing in another hemisphere. I took off in the summer and arrived in the rainy season. I had intentionally chosen a country where the primary language was English, so I at least had that as an anchor. But if I wanted things easy, I could have chosen England. In South Africa, everything was different, from the news media to the food. While the faces around me were various shades of white, brown and Black, I learned that as a tourist from America, I didn't really fit into any of those groups.

The mountains and beaches of South Africa were some of the most beautiful I've ever beheld, but the dichotomy of poverty and wealth in the townships was jarring. I saw folks living in worse conditions than the poor, rural environment where I grew up. The shanty towns were a jumble of sheds with dirt floors shared by several families, and right across the street were first-world homes that rivaled American luxury.

My first host family initially seemed like a good fit. They were an elderly couple, and having spent so much time around older folks when I was growing up, I knew I would be spoiled with good food and pampered with all the comforts I was accustomed to. However, the cultural differences were extreme. This couple was white and of Afrikaner heritage, and it became clear to me that they were still tied to the traditions and mores of the old apartheid class system. I was open-minded, but I didn't think I could stomach hearing my hosts speak of people who looked a lot like me as "the blacks," and blame them for their personal woes. Even watching the news together was a challenge! We eventually agreed that the BBC was neutral enough ground, but I decided to move to a different home.

At the new host's house, I felt more at ease and less distracted by the stresses of racial conflict. He was a doctor and had more progressive views. I also had my own space and could come and go as I pleased. I had my independence and a little money from a living stipend, and I found a local restaurant on the beach where I could expand my culinary palate: I ordered mussels and sherry wine every day (I was only 19, but the legal drinking age was 18 in South Africa), feeling like the grown-up world citizen I was becoming. The cliché "the world is your oyster" really took on a new meaning for me during this time.

I poured my passion and whole self into learning about South Africa. Remember, this was pre-Obama, so to live in a country where there were Black people in power and running the government was inspiring. I visited the jail cell on Robben Island, just north of Cape Town, where Mandela spent 18 of his 27 years in prison. I had been so inspired by his leadership and that of Archbishop Desmond Tutu, and I wanted to take home their spirit of creating a lasting legacy through doing good works.

I was also impressed with the spirit of entrepreneurship I found in South Africa. I had packed a fair amount of candy with me, and in addition to teaching and tutoring math in a local school, I helped locals set up sweet shops to share my passion for business skills and real-world math. I left South Africa with a deeper understanding of the value of community impact in the world. As different as our cultures and ways of life might be, humanity is the same everywhere.

## ...TO ATLANTA...

Going into my senior year as a Morehead-Cain scholar, I had another decision to make. That summer's enrichment opportunity was known as "Internship Summer," and it was designed to teach workplace etiquette, develop professional experience, foster relationships and help students determine their possible career path.

My college roommate, Mahlon (AKA M-Dot), had come to UNC to play football, but he was raised in Atlanta. M-Dot's mom, Maria (AKA, Mama-Dot) graciously opened her home to me, inviting me to live with her during my internship. I liked the idea that Atlanta was just a short drive away from home, but it would still give me an opportunity to stretch my boundaries and expand my comfort zones. And M-Dot and Maria treated me like family.

I came to learn that M-Dot, Mama-Dot and the entire Carey family were on their own *Long Walk to Freedom*. After M-Dot's older brother, Marlin, was awarded All-American honors, life hit their family hard. Like a lot of young people, including myself, Marlin found himself in a bad situation, making unwise choices with the wrong people. He went from scholar to serving up four life sentences *plus* 49 years for the stupid things he'd done as a youngster. My family and I had our own experience with incarceration in the family when my biological dad was in prison. We learned, as Mama-Dot would discover, that only God can truly fill the void of losing a family member to the criminal justice system. But sometimes God gives us His Spirit in the form of people who help us to CEO Life while navigating the devastating prison process as a family.

In the years between college and now, I have stayed closely connected to M-Dot and Mama-Dot, and I consider them family.

In fact, Mama-Dot eventually became *my* executive assistant and we worked side by side for years. I witnessed her passionate fight to keep her son, and their journey to his eventual freedom.

Over time, laws change. When that happens, anything is possible—and in Marlin's case, a law passed in 2016 that gave him a second chance. First time offenders who had committed a crime before the age of 21 were given a chance to go before a parole board and demonstrate their growth—and Marlin did just that. He showed that he was fully responsible for his mistakes, and he had worked hard during his incarceration to repair his character defects and grow and change.

He convinced the board that he would no longer be a threat to society, and as of this writing, he is a free man. His long walk to freedom has now evolved into an enormous life as a self•*ish* servant, working to inspire others who are creating extraordinary lives out of hardships and challenges. He has channeled his pain into passion for living his life to its fullest and empowering others on a similar journey.

Thanks to Mama-Dot, Atlanta became my home away from home. Toward the end of my college career, I was leaning toward teaching or school administration as a career path. Since Mom had been a teacher, it felt like a good continuation of the family legacy. Through Teach for America, I applied to the KIPP (Knowledge is Power Program) in Atlanta.

Created by two former Teach for America instructors, KIPP is a network of tuition-free public charter schools. Inner-city Atlanta experiences poverty similar to what I saw in South Africa, and because of an extreme lack of resources, educators have a hard time getting kids to meet national standards.

KIPP teachers and schools go the extra mile, putting in longer days, teaching through summer and working closely with students to help close the achievement gap across racial lines. The KIPP mission is "together with families and communities, we create joyful, academically excellent schools that prepare students with the skills and confidence to pursue the paths they choose—college, career and beyond—so they can lead fulfilling lives and build a more just world." Their values were directly in line with mine, and I felt confident that this program was the perfect bridge between my two great passions: teaching and leading.

Atlanta surprised me. Just like in South Africa, I saw people who looked like me in positions of power and leadership, from elected officials to wealthy business owners. I was able to see tangible examples of the future I envisioned for myself. I got lucky with KIPP, as it was led by a UNC alum, David Jernigan. I was offered an internship at KIPP WAYS (West Atlanta Young Scholars) Academy. I was excited to share my experience and passion for learning with my students, and I knew they could relate to me, as we had a lot in common. Coincidentally, this was the summer Atlanta rapper T.I. Clifford Harris released his album *T.I. vs. T.I.P.,* where he artistically explored the transition he was embracing from dope boy to smooth CEO. This was a theme I had in common with the students, and it helped us relate to each other. We'd start each day dissecting and discussing a lyric from the album.

One of the most important lessons I took home from that summer was humility. With my extensive tutoring experience and my high-level math skills, I thought I could be an inspiring teacher and leader from day one—but as it turned out, the interns were supposed to work behind the scenes. In my opinion, decorating bulletin boards wasn't the best use of my time. But I did learn how to delegate, how to prioritize tasks, the importance of developing relationships in the workplace, business etiquette and how to manage my time.

I fell in love with Atlanta, and I was inspired by this city that felt like a mecca of Black success. I saw Black entrepreneurs succeeding in ways I never saw back home. As I considered a move there, opportunities popped up that would make the transition easy. KIPP offered me a teaching position. Also, Maria was an executive assistant at a major Fortune 500 company that had a management development program, so I already had a foot in the door. But I heard another passion calling.

## ...AND BACK TO NORTH CAROLINA

I knew I wanted to educate and serve. I wanted to be a leader, and I also wanted to step up to my responsibility to my family: to continue supporting Memaw and my mom. The teaching position at KIPP paid the same amount I was earning managing the Ben & Jerry's store in Chapel Hill. I wanted to do a hybrid of global community-building and teaching, but what was the best choice to build a foundation for the world I wanted to see? Should I start fresh in Atlanta or stay in North Carolina? How could I answer my calling to teach, become a servant leader and further develop my talent and skills in education while creating a lasting legacy for future generations?

In 2007, I was close to graduating and blessed with a number of possible paths forward. Most of my Morehead-Cain cohorts were heading off to become doctors, lawyers and investment bankers, but I had other ideas. With my experience working for a values-centered company like Ben & Jerry's, and inspired as I was by the thriving Black culture and success that I'd seen in South Africa and Atlanta, I had a new idea brewing: social entrepreneurship. I was ruminating on a business model that involved developing, funding and implementing solutions to social, cultural and environmental issues. I wanted to channel my passion into creating lasting social change and authentic community. That's when I discovered the power and genius of *and*.

*AND*.

Serve *and* lead.

In their book *Built to Last: Successful Habits of Visionary Companies*, authors James C. Collins and Jerry I. Porras wrote:

> *Leaders are really good AND people. They don't succumb to the tyranny of the OR. Think of all the ANDs: Humility AND will. Offer a great place to work AND be rigorous. Passion AND best at AND economic engine. Short term-urgency AND long-term building. Creativity AND discipline. Bullets AND cannonballs. Big bets AND productive paranoia.*

I charged myself with the task of creating and growing a business that could be remarkably successful for myself *and* my community. I thought about how I could be a servant leader at my alma mater, UNC, *and* in my business community, *and* my family *and* in the cities and regions where I lived and worked.

As I began to envision this transformative future, an interesting opportunity presented itself. The owner of my Ben & Jerry's franchise, Jim, decided he wanted to move to New York and change his life and pace. He wanted to sell the Chapel Hill store.

I was 21 years old. No one in my family had ever been a business owner. How would owning an ice cream store connect to my grand vision of a future leading, serving and community building? I had already applied for a teaching job through Teach for America, a competitive, challenging program that places top-performing college talent into the highest needs classrooms across the US—and had been offered a position at Southern High School in Durham. This was an exciting opportunity to put into practice all that I had learned in Atlanta, while staying local and close to my family. It was a once-in-a-lifetime chance to learn as a teacher in these classrooms. Anyone with an affinity to lead would receive the best education by teaching in this two-year program. I couldn't turn it down.

*Could I own* and *run a store* and *teach?*

Embracing the power of *and* was just the beginning of my professional and entrepreneurial journey. I had already been running the Ben & Jerry's store *and* going to college, so maybe owning the business would just be stepping it up a bit—more responsibility *and* more reward. As a manager, I was learning everything about running the store: scheduling, invoicing, ordering, payroll and hiring. I had already gone from scooper to scheduler, and learned the value of every position. Could I do all of those things at once?

I thought back to that poster in my room, with the quote from Dr. King about how a man is made through facing and overcoming challenges. Dr. King stayed in the oppressed South so his good works during the civil rights movement could have the most impact. I remembered how inspired I was by Nelson Mandela and how he transformed an entire country—ending apartheid after decades in a jail cell then going on to have a global impact as the first Black president of his nation. I remembered the feeling of teaching young people in South Africa to become business owners. I thought of Memaw and my mom, raising me without running water, and how their service to my future placed me squarely in this place at this moment, with so many choices and options ahead of me. I thought of my cousin Eric, who saw so much promise in me as a high schooler and mentored me, shaping me into a scholar and teaching me the core value of tenacity. What would he say now?

I picked up the phone and called him. This was the beginning of a new chapter for me. I had burning questions to ask and I couldn't make any big leaps without my primo.

## THERE'S FORTUNE IN THE FOLLOW THROUGH

Who do you call when faced with major decisions and opportunities? When you combine the genius of *and* with the conventional adage, "who, not how," you will find your people. I challenge you to build your tribe of advisors by filling in the blanks below:

*I trust _____ and _____ and ______for advice on (finances, faith, family, fun).*

1. Part of being self•*ish* is the reward of having our cake (and ice cream) and eating it too! What's a passionate area of your life where you feel absolutely torn, indecisive, stuck or unclear? What would having your cake *and* ice cream *and* eating it look like in this part of your life?
2. Can you find the tyranny of "or" in this area? Think of tyranny as a dictator mindset where things are reduced to a strict and often false binary belief. Sometimes it's believing that financial resources won't let you succeed, that time resources hold you back, or listening to other self-limiting thoughts on replay in your head. Instead of holding yourself back with the restrictive "or," what is preventing you from having your cake, your ice cream, and eating it too?
3. You have a choice now to apply more passion ~~or~~ *and* apply the genius of "and." What is it going to be?

@Quoted Visually

# PART II: EXTRA•ORDINARY

*Adjective*:

Origin: Late Middle English: from Latin *extraordinarius,* from *extra ordinem* "outside the normal course of events." Very unusual or remarkable. Unusually great.

# CHAPTER 4
# PASSION$^2$
## SCOOPING YOUR WAY UP

*"There's no passion to be found in playing small, in living a life less than the one we are capable of living."*
—Nelson Mandela

The genius of *and* isn't quite the beginning. Before you can summon the magic of *and,* you have to have the right ingredients. The power of and is more made up of what comes before and than what follows. And that power is fueled by passion.

___ *and* ___ = ?

It's an empty equation. An unfinished formula.

But when it's complete, it's *bold.*

The CEO Life is *bold.* It's audacious. It's filled with passionate commitment to reinventing the status quo. If you want to live *bold,* you have to *ask bold questions and make bold decisions.* And the precursor to *bold questions* is passionate curiosity.

When my friend Jim in Chapel Hill told me he was selling his franchise, I called my primo, Eric. I felt the pressure to make the right decision, and I knew that the result of making the right decision would set me on an extraordinary life path. Everything leading up to now had been extraordinary, so I knew what came next would be, too.

Eric and I were curious, so we asked a bold question:

*What would it take for me to buy this store before I graduate?*

Eric was working as an engineer in Boston. He shared my passion for numbers and we both liked the numbers we got when we did the math for being franchise owners.

*I'm 21 years old. How can I do this?*

I had always made outside-the-box decisions that defied even the Morehead-Cain program's expectations. Winners of a full-ride, four-year scholarship don't usually live at home, and they don't typically have a job. And graduates of the program hadn't historically bought a franchise across the street from the university; they moved on and became doctors, lawyers, bankers and consultants. Then again, most kids from the poor, rural South don't graduate at the top of their class, receive invitations to attend world-class universities and receive distinguished scholarships. But self•*ish* servants who CEO Life must sometimes choose the road less traveled—and often create a path where a road doesn't exist!

No one in my family had ever owned a business, so I didn't have any examples of that kind of success. But I did have access to a vast, global network of experts: the Morehead-Cain alumni network. Alumni go on to mentor, invest and support their fellow scholars with job and internship opportunities, philanthropic support and professional advice. So I leaned on these experts for business advice. I was feverish with a passionate drive. I learned how to write a business plan. I learned how to negotiate lease terms. I learned how to develop relationships with banks so that I improved my chances of securing a loan—after all, I was only 21 and didn't have a lot of credit or capital. I learned how to make an offer and form a partnership. Eric and I created Primo, and in May of 2008, two days before I graduated from college, we bought our first Ben & Jerry's store.

I need to mention that there's such a thing as being *too bold*—

and by that I mean overly ambitious and maybe a little cocky. It's not just important to ask *bold* questions, you also have to ask *quality* questions.

Eric and I were tenacious, and as much as we liked the idea of owning a franchise, we *loved* the idea of owning two! We saw the Durham store on the Duke campus as the perfect partner for our Chapel Hill store, so we pursued both at the same time. We applied for a $500,000 loan from the bank and pursued our goal relentlessly. In the end, we learned another valuable lesson: asking for more means if you only get some, it will turn out to be enough.

The bank turned us down for that massive loan. *But.* They *would* give us a $50,000 loan, which was enough to help us buy the Chapel Hill franchise. When you shoot for the moon, even if you miss, you're with the stars.

When you shoot for the moon

Even if you miss, you're with the stars

The third lesson here was about experience. As newbies in the franchising world, we lacked the experience to ask the right questions. Our questions were indeed *bold* (Can we borrow $500,000?) but they weren't specific enough about that second store. They weren't *quality* questions. We saw something shiny: a successful store on another university campus—what could go wrong? It turned out being denied that massive loan was a gift.

There were problems with the lease and the store was distressed in ways we didn't see. If we had bought that second store, the math would have been about seven times the work of a single store, and would have destroyed us before Primo even got started.

Now that we had asked bold questions and made bold decisions, I was able to experience the magic and genius of *and.*

I could be of service *and* be a successful business owner. I accepted the teaching job in Durham, teaching precalculus and honors math Monday through Friday, then I ran the store on the weekends. During the peak summer season when teachers have time off, I could put all my energy into the store. Just as I had split up my week between Memaw's house and UNC all through college, juggling my days to maximize my time, I built a bridge between my two passions. I had bought into a global brand, and I got busy reimagining and maximizing the store's potential.

Some people are creators, some are inventors and some are improvers: folks who can see something in its raw form and imagine how it can be better. Ben Cohen and Jerry Greenfield did this with ice cream. You can get ice cream anywhere, but when it's made with the best ingredients, unique and imaginative flavors, and you create a business model with a foundation of social justice and community-building, the result is better than any other scoop. Ben and Jerry asked what I was now asking myself about my franchise: *how can I make it better so that it also benefits my community?*

The first thing I did was keep the store open past 9 pm. We were in a college town with one of the country's oldest universities right across the street. By shutting down early, we were cutting off a connection to that school and the student body. I expanded the store's business hours to match student schedules, accommodating student night life—we stayed open until the clubs closed down! What do a bunch of drunk kids want on their walk back to the dorms? A late night snack! Unfortunately, staying open *that* late meant our staff quickly had a lot of extra cleaning to do, dealing with puddles of sick and unruly, intoxicated customers. We eventually found our sweet spot, staying open until 1 am.

We changed the music that we played, making it more inviting for a young, hip crowd. We changed the lighting at night, creating a mood. We hosted theme nights. We improved the signage, making the store more visible: by simply adding a giant ice cream cone, we attracted more international students and became a prime spot for tourists. We put in outside seating and umbrellas.

We plugged into the University, setting up comprehensive partnerships with student organizations. We partnered with the UNC Dance Marathon, connected with the campus YMCA, set up ice cream stands for on-campus events, asking local organizations to host their events at our store in exchange for a percentage of proceeds. We created the Vermonster Contest, 20 scoops of ice cream, four brownies, cookies, bananas and toppings—then we sold it for fifty dollars and held a contest to see who could eat it faster. We donated ice cream for student orientation, making connections with students from day one.

We were thinking big, creating ties with our community and developing authentic relationships. Because we asked the *bold question,* "How can we make the store better and benefit our community," we increased our sales by 26 percent in our first year. Another really important thing happened at the end of that year of Primo owning our first Ben & Jerry's: my daughter Nia was conceived.

During my first year as a business owner *and* a teacher, I had the bandwidth to excel at both. But as I was wrapping up the second year of my teaching commitment with Teach for America, I had to ask myself a bold new question: *How can I continue to lead, be a business owner and the father I want to be?*

While I loved my time in the classroom and had made some of the most impactful relationships of my life, I discovered that my business could actually *be* my classroom. I could use my business as a vehicle for true community change *and* servant leadership.

## WHAT ARE CATTLE GUARDS?

In 2011, I put all my efforts into scaling the Primo business. I got a call from the UNC business school—they had about 300 MBA candidates coming in for their orientation and they wanted to connect with the shop somehow, but not bring them to the store. They would pay us $1000 a day for three days to scoop ice cream. How could I bring the store to them?

This is when I learned that my store could be an omnichannel. By investing in the right equipment, I could stop relying on our brick and mortar business for profit. Instead, I could expand by bringing ice cream to events: games, celebrations, clubs, the campus...suddenly the playing ground got a whole lot bigger, and every square mile of Chapel Hill was up for grabs. But I was curious. I asked a bold question:

*Why just Chapel Hill?*

When we bought the store, I was led to believe that I only had rights to this area. I couldn't leave Chapel Hill due to a non-compete clause. I took this limitation at face value and never questioned it. I didn't dare dip into other territories because I didn't want to create problems in my business.

Cattle guards are mental limitations. They are barriers we are told to believe in without research or questions. When ranchers have livestock, they put holes in the ground to establish a perimeter. Baby cows' legs get stuck in those holes if they try to wander too far, and so they are programmed from a young age not to walk that far. As they grow up to become raging bulls with large hooves, those mental limitations are still in place, even if they could step right over the holes without any injury. When I was a kid, and right up until about 10 years ago, I had one of the meanest underbites you've ever seen in your life. You may be asking why I didn't just get it fixed. We brushed our teeth by putting water in a coffee mug and dipping the toothbrush in—our budget was for essentials only back then, and the dentist wasn't essential.

There was one time I did go to the dentist because a 6'9", 375-pound teammate fell on my head while diving for a loose ball in basketball and broke one of my front teeth. I asked the dentist then if I could one day get braces to fix my smile, and he told me he'd have to break my jaw in order to ever get rid of the enormous underbite. So I walked around all during college, and my initial business years, smiling real big with crooked teeth and an underbite. But God has a way of winking at us sometimes.

I'll never forget, a local orthodontist named Dr. Smith booked us to do an ice cream party at his office, and we formed a friendship. One day we were hanging out, and he worked up the courage to ask me if I would let him fix my smile. I went on to educate him on how he'd have to break my jaw and I didn't really want to go through all of that. Dr. Smith couldn't stop laughing because over the course of those 20 years, orthodontics had grown by leaps and bounds, and something called "Invisalign" could take care of the issue painlessly. You see? Cattle guards.

Back in 2011 when I was interested in expanding my business territory, my curiosity was piqued and I put in a few calls. The first one was to the city of Chapel Hill to find out about business restrictions. Then I called Ben & Jerry's corporate headquarters and asked about the non-compete clause I had heard about. It turned out that the city and county lines were only cattle guards! There was nothing holding us back, and we could spread out to the entire Triangle area of North Carolina—an area centered around Raleigh, Durham and Chapel Hill, containing three of the state's largest cities and three major universities: Duke, North Carolina State University and UNC-Chapel Hill.

By asking bold questions, we expanded our off-premise sales beyond our expectations. Primo was hitting that sweet spot of impact *and* ROI, impacting those who worked within our company *and* in the community. By 2015, Primo was recognized as the number one off-premise sales leader for Ben & Jerry's.

Cattle guards can be anything from where you live to what you can have and what you can achieve: cars, homes, neighborhoods or schools. They can be about money you can earn, policies, rules, races and people. But they can be reimagined, and in doing so, you're removing your own self-limiting beliefs. When you have child-like curiosity, you'll ask bold questions, make bold decisions and remove every type of limitation: mental, emotional, physical and professional.

But asking bold questions and making bold decisions requires decisiveness, confidence and endurance. Success comes from practice, experience and taking risks that pay off. The quality of your questions matters just as much as their boldness. Here's a short list of bold questions you can ask yourself:

*What's the worst that can happen?*
*If money wasn't an issue, what would I do?*
*If this (policy, rule, barrier) wasn't an issue, I would be able to…?*

Cattle guards are often outdated, illusory or the result of someone else's fears or failures. Sometimes they're cultural, such as the notion that another person's beliefs or background will impede a good working relationship with them. When Primo bought that first store in Chapel Hill, I connected with the "Ice Cream Queen." Karen had been pushing the Ben & Jerry's envelope for decades. She and her husband Robert started buying franchises in the late 1990s, and when she unexpectedly lost her husband, she had four young sons at home and 15 stores. With unwavering tenacity, Karen stepped in and stepped up to create an extraordinary business and life for her kids.

Karen and I were polar opposites, and had little in common besides our business vision. On face value, what would I have to talk about with this affluent, older white mother of four nearing retirement age? But we looked beyond the cattle guards, saw something in each other and enjoyed spending time together despite our differences. Years later, in 2017, Primo was forming a board of advisors, and Karen was at the top of my list of invitees. She helped Primo build and grow its portfolio beyond all of our expectations.

By 2022, Karen had remarried and moved from Washington, DC to Tennessee and was ready for retirement and her next phase of life. She sold off 19 stores, but had three remaining, and they were some of the top stores in the system. Primo was her first choice to take over those three gems. We jumped at the opportunity, but knew we had big shoes to fill.

One primary value for Primo is growth. How could we grow stores that were already wildly successful? Hadn't they already reached their full potential? We looked closely at the National Harbor store. Its location wasn't central to tourist attractions. There was an enormous ferris wheel in town, and all the main stores were on the other side of it. There was a central tourism booth, but our store was off the beaten path. What Karen said was gospel, and she told us that no matter what, there was no way to improve that store's visibility.

But I asked a bold question: what about changing the signage? What if we put a cartoonishly enormous, neon ice cream cone at the top of the building? Maybe that was going too far, but I found out that National Harbor had its own jurisdiction to approve signage. Most cities wouldn't approve big, bold and unconventional signs, but after pitching the right ideas to the right people, spending six figures on the exterior of the store and adding a tie-dye mural, bold and eye-catching benches out front and LED signage, by our 12-month anniversary we had increased business by 39 percent.

The Old Town Alexandria shop, the oldest one in DC, is in a part of the city known for needing historical society approval for *everything.* Like the National Harbor store, it's located off the main street with little visibility. I asked the city about signage, and was told of their strict "no signs, no murals policy" as they want all storefronts and facades to respect the neighborhood's heritage. I checked all the cattle guards, and eventually found the right person on the right board to help us improve our visibility. It turned out that there was a new initiative around art and artists in the community, and if the proposed mural fit the community's spirit, it would be possible to implement. As of this writing, a week ago, our proposal was approved for a remarkable new signage and mural combination—one that elevates and celebrates the community, the environment *and* attracts new customers to our store.

Cattle guards prevent livestock from crossing into another area where they don't belong, but they don't have to be barriers between you and your goals or dreams. Look closely at your life circumstances and ask yourself where you feel limited, and I'm guessing you'll discover some barriers and boundaries that can be challenged by asking bold questions and making bold decisions.

## THERE'S FORTUNE IN THE FOLLOW THROUGH

Remember, cattle guards can be about anything: money, policies, rules, races and people. But they can be removed and reimagined. Success comes from practice and experience, and taking risks that pay off. Stay curious and cultivate your confidence, one bold question at a time.

1. What is one "cattle guard" that keeps you from your CEO Life right now?
2. What is one bold question you could ask that might constructively challenge this cattle guard?
3. Raise your "passion lid." Connecting back to your values, dreams and having your cake and ice cream, make one *big* decision right now that your future self will look back and thank you for.

# CHAPTER 5
# STRATEGY + FOCUS

## MICROSCOPES, TELESCOPES + KALEIDOSCOPES

> *"Your main thing is to keep your main thing the main thing."*
> —Steven Covey, author of *7 Habits of Highly Effective People*

Focus is strategy. Whatever the obstacle you are facing in your life or business, there is always a strategy to solve the problem. The solution is in how you focus. Where your focus goes, your energy flows—then everything grows.

The flame on a candle can barely light a room, but *focused* light, such as a laser, can cut through steel. When you apply this concept of focus to solving your problems, you will find remarkable results. We use the word "light" in a lot of ways: it literally helps us to see, and we figuratively shed light on a subject to reveal what it's made of.

Now, let's look at the word "scope." One definition of scope is "the extent of the area or subject matter that something deals with or to which it is relevant." We can focus our intention, our energy, our light through various scopes, such as a microscope, a telescope or a kaleidoscope. In a minute, I'm going to give you some specific examples of how to look at problems through these different lenses, but let's talk a bit about these scopes first.

## SCOPES

A microscope helps us to focus on a finite area. We examine a minuscule thing, or a very small part of the problem in order to see it clearly. Using a microscope, we can look intensely at something as small as a single cell—one of the building blocks of life! The lenses on a microscope bend light towards our eyes, magnifying the object and making it appear larger than it actually is so we can see all its minute parts.

We can apply this principle to problem-solving by thinking in terms of aiming our focus to shed light on all the small, intricate details that make up a problem. What is its origin? What events led to the problem? What events led to those events? What decisions were made that caused those events? What actions were taken or not taken that brought us to this result? What is the impact of this problem—what are all the ways that the results we are inspecting affect our business, our goals, our lives? Taking a microscopic view, a microscopic *focus* on the problem is the best way to analyze where we are today.

Now let's talk about a telescope—the tool that amateur stargazers and astronomers alike use to focus in on something distant can't be seen with the naked eye. Telescopes focus light through lenses and use mirrors to concentrate that light, allowing us to bring a distant object into clear view. Using a telescope, we can see stars, nebulas and galaxies. We know those celestial bodies are there, but without a telescope, we have no way of seeing them clearly.

Using a telescopic focus on our problems allows us to look far out in the future, shedding light on the *big* picture. While the *micro*scopic view helps us see all the small details of our problem, the *tele*scopic view allows us to focus on things like goals, growth and the broader impact of the problem. How is the current problem impacting our goals? How will it impact our community? We use a telescopic lens to keep our long-term business and life goals in focus and to try to determine the ultimate results of every small action we're taking today.

There's also a third scope: the kaleidoscope. A kaleidoscopic view allows us to look at something ordinary and to see it totally differently. It distorts our focus. Kaleidoscopes are devices that use tilted mirrors to reflect light, creating a patterned view of an object, and as we turn the kaleidoscope, the mirrors change angles, capturing a different part of what we're inspecting. Interestingly, the word "kaleidoscope" is a Greek word made of three parts: *kalos* meaning beauty; *eidos* meaning the form or shape that is seen; and *skopeo,* which means to examine. If you put that all together it means "observation of beautiful forms."

A kaleidoscopic view allows us to take a whole different approach to our problem. It changes our vantage point as the lens and mirrors shift, so that we may be looking at the same thing but we're seeing it differently. It's kind of a magical view: it turns the problem on its head, twisting and changing it, allowing us to see its angles and aspects in new ways that we couldn't possibly perceive through a microscope or a telescope—and definitely not with our naked eye. The problem becomes a mosaic of color and angles previously impossible to imagine.

Another way of thinking of the kaleidoscopic view is to consider a rainbow. When we see a rainbow here on Earth, it's an arc. But a rainbow seen from outer space is a full circle. What happens when you look at a rainbow through a kaleidoscope? It's an ever-changing pattern of light and color. So is your problem. When we apply a kaleidoscopic focus, we see all new angles, parts, solutions and possible outcomes.

## STRATEGY

We can use our various focus lenses as different types of strategies to solve our problems. Let's pivot away from rainbows and mosaics and talk about focus in terms of warfare. The reason I think this example works is because when you're tackling a problem, your ultimate goal is to win. You may be battling yourself—your self-limiting beliefs, your confidence, your readiness, your skills or feeling like you're in a rut. Or, you may be battling something external—a court case, financial challenges, competing businesses or employee management. Whether your problem is inside or outside, chances are you feel like you're at war and you need to win this battle in order to succeed.

In the warfare analogy, we have two ways to focus: strategic and tactical. With strategic focus, you're looking through the scope on a gun, aiming at a target far away. There's that telescopic view again: it's the big picture, the broad goals, the end result you want. You are a sniper, sighting a distant target.

When you take a strategic view, you're looking at a distant target—maybe it's a growth goal, a financial goal or a personal goal. What far away place are you trying to get to?

In terms of my business, the strategic focus through a telescopic lens means taking a step *back* and asking myself, "Where am I taking this business? What is my 10-year target? What is the three-year picture? How can I strategize the upcoming year to meet that three-year milestone? What about the next six months, three months, 30 days and one week? What about tomorrow?" The strategic view is planning, mapping and aligning today's, tomorrow's, and next week's actions so that I can prepare to hit every target—while keeping those *big picture* goals in focus.

The next type of focus in this warfare example is tactical. While the strategic focus is like a sniper's view, the tactical focus is a knife fight. It's dealing with what's immediately around you with intention and awareness. In a knife fight, all the contact is up-close and personal, and to succeed, you have to be fully present, right there in the moment—you can't be thinking about or looking at anything besides what is in the here and now.

This is how you focus on a specific, short-term problem that you're trying to overcome. With tactical focus, I'm not thinking of tomorrow, next week, next month or next year; I'm thinking about how I can make moves and pivot *right now*, today, to solve the immediate challenge.

Another example of these two types of focus—strategic and tactical—is triage. In a war zone (or an accident site, hospital or any medical emergency), the medical professionals must think quickly and prioritize every injury. The tactical focus in a triage situation is turning first to the victims about to bleed out: you have to stop that bleeding before they die. The strategic focus allows you to take on injuries like a dislocated shoulder or abrasions—yes, they need attention and care, but it's not as urgent. In terms of care, the first step with a wound is tactical: stop the bleeding. The strategic focus is the operation required to save that life.

I'm going to give you some real-life examples of a few major obstacles I've encountered as an entrepreneur on the way to CEO Life. You'll see how I used the microscopic, telescopic and kaleidoscopic lenses, as well as strategic and tactical focus to overcome these problems so I could continue to help my businesses succeed and grow.

Keep this in mind as you read: in most business and life problems, you can start with the strategic (big picture) view with a telescopic lens (bringing the future into focus), then the microscopic lens (to see the problem up close), followed by the kaleidoscopic lens (to observe every side of the problem) and finally the tactical focus that allows you to be in the moment so you solve the immediate, most urgent part of the problem. Once you've creatively solved those up-close and in-the-moment problems, you can then move forward to strategize your movements, decisions and actions to reach more distant goals.

## OBSTACLE 1: HOW CAN I MAKE MORE MONEY WITH A SEASONAL BUSINESS?

Ben & Jerry's has a phenomenal product. These days, you can find specialty ice creams and desserts in the grocery store, but believe me when I tell you that Ben & Jerry's were first. While other ice cream stores gave you a choice in flavors, Ben & Jerry's product has always had primo ingredients, imaginative and unique flavor combinations and a superior customer experience.

When we started our company, Primo, with our first Ben & Jerry's franchise, I discovered that ice cream is a seasonal product. In some markets, like Florida and California, people will probably eat ice cream year-round. But in areas with a cooler fall and winter climate, business really dies down. I looked at the summer numbers, and I looked at the winter numbers, and I decided the problem was the seasons. How could I solve the seasonal problem?

My first big off-site partnership was with Tanger, the outlet mall company. At outlet malls, once the retail spaces are ready, only the big-ticket stores have the resources for opening their stores right away. So if you're Coach, Polo or Nike, you've got the capital to set up that store and hit the ground running, making money that first day. But restaurants face a different issue: they have build-outs. That raw space may be ready, but they need a kitchen, a counter, a floor plan and a flow to keep customers happy.

For Tanger's big grand opening, the restaurants and food vendors weren't ready. When I met with their representative, she explained this unique problem to me and I had a unique solution: I could bring in a satellite setup as a mobile vendor.

I brought in a beautiful cart and set up a portable shop, selling scoops left, right and center. People were lining up for our scoops all day, and the business relationship with Tanger became long-term—we're still doing deals with this company today. But I noticed something right from the start: there were only a few of us set up as portable food vendors. Aside from our ice cream, there was lemonade, a popcorn cart and Auntie Anne's pretzels.

Let me tell you about that pretzel line. The smell of those pretzels was bringing people from blocks away to form a line 50 to 60 people deep *all day.* There was something really special about Auntie Anne's product and sellability. And they definitely had one thing that we didn't have at our Ben & Jerry's store: they weren't seasonal.

Around this time, Ben & Jerry's corporate reached out to let me know that it was time to update the shop's decor—after all, it was now over twenty years old, with the original black and white tiles on the floor like a checkered flag. They required that we do some cosmetic updates, so I was mapping out my plans for a remodel. Those cosmetic updates weren't just slapping paint on the walls—we had to redo the floors and signage. It wasn't a small job, and remodels cost money!

I started to think about how casinos and airports had co-location and co-branding of two stores under one roof. I had a colleague who was operating a Ben & Jerry's and Wetzel's Pretzels in the same store, and it seemed to be a successful operation. These co-location spaces seemed to work very well, and I thought it could be the solution to my seasonal problem.

At my Franklin Street store in Chapel Hill, I had about 1,400 square feet of usable space, which was plenty of room to open a second business. So I imagined half the store dedicated to Ben & Jerry's, and the other half selling Auntie Anne's pretzels, solving my seasonal sales slump problem and expanding my earning potential to a year-round model.

I contacted Auntie Anne's headquarters, traveled to Lancaster, Pennsylvania to complete the corporate training procedures, went through the approval process and got permission to franchise. In January of 2012, Jerry Greenfield himself (of Ben & Jerry's fame) came to our grand opening.

I used up our family savings to make this investment, and the space looked beautiful. The college kids were hungry, and I was ready to feed them 12 months out of the year. I have never worked so hard as I did in the next year to lose $100,000—but that wasn't all. While I was losing money at my store, I was also embroiled in a lawsuit (more on that in a moment).

What followed this catastrophe was a period of such darkness in my life, I didn't think I could ever see the light. I had always been a hard worker, an exemplary performer and someone my teammates could rely on—in my work life, in my athletic life and in my family life. I felt like I had let everyone down, and my drive and ambitious focus shifted so that all I could see was my failure.

I had no telescopic view—I only had a microscopic view, and it was trained on my mistakes. If I was using a kaleidoscope, I was examining myself as a total failure from every possible angle. My self-worth as an entrepreneur plummeted. And while the low season of my business set in, my seasonal depression got worse. For three weeks, I stayed in bed. I didn't see the point in getting up to face all the problems, both micro and macro, that I was confronting.

One thing I undoubtedly did right in my life was marrying Katie. We are partners in every sense of the word. She and our kids have been a part of our business-building from the beginning. When she saw me turn the corner and go down that dark alley to get into a knife fight with *myself,* she knew how to speak my love languages: acts of service and tangible gifts.

The first gift she gave me (other than her unwavering love and support), was a pair of Air Jordan—21s. (If you know, then you know.) Yeah, I put them on, but I didn't feel any better. I didn't believe my feet deserved to walk in those shoes.

But the second gift she gave me was transformative, and it's proof that great things come in small packages. This gift was what ultimately led me to change my focus. She gave me a telescope, a microscope and a kaleidoscope made out of 100 percent cotton. She had a custom T-shirt made for me with a quote from one of my favorite, most inspirational entrepreneur-CEOs, Shawn Carter, AKA Jay-Z:

*The genius thing we did was we didn't give up.*

I wore those shoes and that shirt every day for a month straight to keep me inspired and motivated, and to remind me to change my focus. I could be the smartest person in the world, an absolute genius. But if I gave up on myself, it wouldn't mean a thing. The way that shirt transformed me led to me rebuilding Primo and getting back on track mentally, emotionally and financially.

In Chapter 7, we're going to dive into the concept of "asking quality questions." For now, let me just say that when I was focusing on my problems, the telescopic view led me to ask, "How can I move from being a seasonal business to making money year-round?" The microscopic view was on my earnings in the winter months. But that view was too narrow—it needed to be turned and reflected and run through that kaleidoscopic lens until it became the *quality question* I really needed to be asking, which was, *"How do I sell more ice cream when it counts?"*

If I know I make my money during certain months out of the year, how can I make *more money* during those months to help sustain my business the rest of the year? And using that strategic view, what can I do during the down months to prepare for the high months? What can be done in December to help blow my April through September earnings out of the water?

The highest professional performers who live the most extraordinary lives have seasonal moments. Every athlete has a down season. What do they do during those off months? They train and prepare themselves for the regular season. They strategize how they can improve their performance, build their muscles, increase their flexibility, out-perform their competitors. They study the competition; they study themselves. They work with trainers who are familiar with cutting-edge physiology studies. They repair injuries and learn how to avoid them next time. And sometimes they even plan for what they'll do when their athletic careers inevitably come to an end.

The top surgeons in the world need laser-sharp focus for every operation—but during their downtime, they're updating their knowledge. They're reading the latest studies and attending week-long conferences about cutting-edge technologies and scientific findings. They're learning about the latest discoveries of their peers. Surgery requires microscopic focus, but they're using telescopic and kaleidoscopic views as well to improve their knowledge base and maintain their skills between procedures.

Dan Sullivan is known as the Strategic Coach. Since 1988, he and his wife Babs Smith have been developing entrepreneurs to help them reach their potential. One important topic he tackles is time management, with his concept of The Entrepreneurial Time System. Business-building isn't all about grinding out ways to make money every single day. He breaks down how to get the best results by shifting your focus from "all work, all day, every day" to "free days, focus days and buffer days."

Free days are exactly what they sound like: a day off. You're not working, you're not reading or monitoring those work emails, you're not jumping on conference calls or reviewing your marketing materials. You're playing. You're spending time with your family. You're practicing your hobby. You're giving your brain a deserved break from that entrepreneurial laser focus (remember, laser focus can cut through steel. Should you be looking at your kids with that focus?)

Focus days are also straightforward: spend them building your business. You're using all your perspectives—your telescope view, your microscope view and your kaleidoscope view—to run your business and make money. You're putting that marketing plan into action. You're on a call in the middle of that knife fight, making moves.

Then there are the buffer days. This is when you're doing all the administrative work that goes into preparing you for that knife fight. You're printing out the yearly projections, you're studying the numbers, designing the website—everything you need to keep operations running smoothly.

When it came to solving what I *thought* was Primo's problem

—how to make a seasonal store a year-round money-maker—I ended up throwing all of my money at the wrong issue. It was like the battle was in Antarctica but I attacked Canada instead. They both have snow, right? I was looking at the globe instead of the country I should have been focused on—or rather, I was looking at the wrong months. Those cold months weren't where I could maximize my potential; it was the summer months all along. Those winter months were my buffer months. Spring and summer were my focus months. That's where my energy should have been directed.

This leads me back to my favorite saying of Steven Covey's: *Your main thing is to keep your main thing your main thing.* My main thing was ice cream. Pretzels were never my main thing. I saw something shiny—that long line at the Auntie Anne's pretzel shop—and got distracted from my main thing. I should have been focused on how to make my already long line even longer with what I had right in front of me. My strategic goal was for Primo to become the top ice cream contractor in the world, with more sales than anyone else. I couldn't do that if I shifted my focus to pretzels!

So to climb out of my dark hole of despair and seasonal depression, I applied those different scopes and found a solution that aligned with a new and refined strategy. I traveled to other top-performing Ben & Jerry's stores looking for growth.

I visited a store in Greensboro, North Carolina which, back in 2011 before the Auntie Anne's detour, I had been thinking of buying. At the time, the franchise owner wasn't interested in selling. But wouldn't you know it? Timing is everything. The owner had just been presented with a life-changing opportunity to pursue another dream, and he needed to divest from his Ben & Jerry's ownership quickly. This meant that Primo was able to present a new deal, at half my original offer. Not only did he want a quick transition, he knew that with the capital I was giving him, he didn't have to deal with the banks or financing.

Primo now owned two stores, one in Chapel Hill and one in

Greensboro. But our off-site business ventures with the mobile ice cream operation at the Tanger Outlets made in one month what the stores made in three—in part because there was no overhead. This made for some magical math: With two stores and the off-site business, Primo now owned the equivalent of three stores: 1+1=3. And Primo kept growing. Our company, which had struggled to do $200,000 in one year, was now selling more than one million every year.

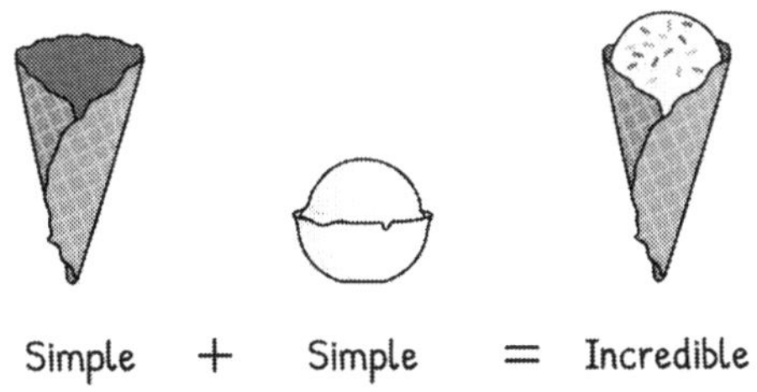


## OBSTACLE 2: THE LAWSUIT

Over the years, whenever I had a little bit of extra cash, I would buy up some sort of property (more on this in Chapter 6). Usually these were foreclosures, short sales, small rental properties or remote parcels of land with timber tracts for harvesting into lumber that could be sold off—properties under $10,000. In 2012, I was fresh out of college and was ready to step up my game to the big leagues and buy something commercial.

I came across a good deal to buy a dilapidated commercial

building with the roof caved in. It had a little house and some land that came with it, too. I knew the building needed some work, so I had contractors look at it, and one contractor gave me a bid so low, it seemed too good to be true. It *was* too good to be true.

When they finished the job, I paid them the agreed upon fee, about $75,000. Then they sent me another bill demanding $50,000 more. I argued that we had a fixed price contract—they couldn't just bill me extra. It would be one thing if we were five or ten grand off, but they were asking for $50,000! I was still green—where was I going to come up with that? Keep in mind, this was all going on at the *same time* Primo was renovating our Chapel Hill Ben & Jerry's store, as well as adding in the Auntie Anne's pretzels.

One thing led to another, and we couldn't settle our dispute, so we ended up in court. I beat the lawsuit; the judge threw it out. Even though I had spent a lot of money on a lawyer, I was relieved that it was over. But the contractor decided to appeal the judge's decision. Here we go again. This time, we got an older, retired judge, with a reputation dating back to the Jim Crow era, and we saw that we didn't have a fighting chance. He ruled in her favor and granted her the $50,000, plus legal fees and interest. All in, it was about $100,000.

Needless to say, I felt like I'd been discriminated against. Plus, I had just lost $100,000 on the pretzel deal, and now I had a $100,000 lien attached to my real estate business and the commercial building. You can understand how I ended up in a deep, dark hole of depression, unable to see the light—and you need light to focus through any kind of lens.

But then I got a superpower: my Jordans and my T-shirt.

*The genius thing we did was we didn't give up.*

Eventually, I found somebody to buy the pretzel equipment for $25,000—a long way from the $100,000 I needed, but it was a start. Then I met with my accountant, who helped me shift my focus. She told me that the $75,000 loss would be effectively reduced to $50,000 once we filed my taxes and I got the hardship write-off. A little more light was coming into view—and then, I found a grant program to help entrepreneurs rebound from failed businesses.

I started out focusing only on my resentment, fear and failures. As some of you know, being the victim of racial discrimination is at the very least distracting, and at worst devastating—emotionally and spiritually. Because I was looking at what felt like the destruction of my business, I was allowing my focus to be pulled from the *real* problem: where was this money going to come from?

Once I saw my strategic goal with the telescopic lens—rebuilding Primo and recouping my losses—I was able to look through the microscopic lens at each and every dollar I had to make. Then, by using the kaleidoscope, I was able to turn the problem around and look at it from every angle—and the solutions presented themselves. Now I began to see the solutions: tax relief and repositioning the asset. Bad stuff is going to happen. But even though this bad thing happened, I shifted focus and saved my shirt. Or actually, it was the shirt that saved me.

## OBSTACLE 3: 2020 AND THE PANDEMIC

This next example requires a jump forward in time. By the year 2018, I had scaled Primo to five Ben & Jerry's stores: in Chapel Hill, Greensboro and Raleigh, North Carolina; one in Atlanta and one in Melbourne, Florida. In addition to that, our off-premise business was going wild with major music festivals, sporting events like the ACC Men's and Women's Basketball Tournaments and special and private events. We clustered our events close together so we could do several in one week. We had found our niche, and we were doing Ben & Jerry's sales outside four walls better than anybody.

Primo was big enough that we could bring Eric on full time to take care of all the jobs that were his area of strength (and definitely not mine): the detail-oriented, time-sensitive tasks like insurance and taxes. By 2019, we were ready to scale up like never before. We closed that year with drive, vision and momentum.

At the start of 2020, we had all of our new development agreements signed for new territory growth in Texas and Florida, and our off-site special and sporting events were our bread and butter. We saw the value of investing in our top-notch team of leaders for development and coaching, and in February of that year, we took them all on a four-day management trip in the Everglades and an Outward Bound leadership retreat. We had plans for 2020.

But 2020 had plans for us.

I don't have to explain to you how the global pandemic hit the service industry. But this is where focus comes in. I remembered a quote that has been attributed to Winston Churchill: "During times of crisis, bad companies fail, good companies survive and great companies improve." I knew we were a strong company, destined to be even better. Primo made the decision to focus our telescopic lens on growth and to use these challenging times to go into *greatness.*

Instead of firing all of those wonderful managers we had been developing, we saw them for what they really were: the backbone of our company. With that new perspective, the closed stores meant that we had more time to do additional leadership training.

We also discovered that this was a great time to buy up suffering businesses from owners who were (rightfully) afraid of the unknown. Primo developed a reputation as the company you call when you need to get out of your business quickly—we could get the deal done. We got calls from Chicago, Illinois and St. Louis, Missouri. We bought up a franchise in our first tourist location, Chattanooga, Tennessee, across from The Passage (the first stop on the historic Trail of Tears), and near the Tennessee Aquarium. Then we bought a franchise in Athens, Georgia. Because of the pandemic, we bought all these franchises for less than *half* of what they would have cost a year before.

With Primo's strategic focus on unprecedented growth and our tactical focus on tackling individual markets, we went from five franchises to nine—and then to double digits. As we looked around for stores to add to Primo's portfolio, we didn't have to focus on the problem stores that were suffering. Instead, we bought up the stores that had been around for years.

Also, because many of the Ben & Jerry's stores had opened in the 1980s, these owners were getting ready to retire. Their stores were in prime locations, and we ended up buying franchises in Washington, DC; Asheville and Charlotte, North Carolina; and Savannah, Georgia. While our off-premise sales had tanked as a result of the pandemic (and would take years to return), Primo's franchise ownership exceeded our wildest expectations, and today we have two dozen operating units.

Being in the Southeast during Covid gave us a bit of an unfair competitive edge. While much of the country remained shut down, the rebellious South stayed open (for better or worse), and our stores in Texas, Georgia, North Carolina and Florida had record years in 2021. With our telescopic and strategic focus on world-class hospitality, our microscopic and tactical focus is on developing managers and cultivating our stores. We have achieved greatness because we look at our problems through the kaleidoscopic lens, which helps us pivot and change our vantage point through every type of challenge we can imagine (and even through the ones we can't).

## THERE'S FORTUNE IN THE FOLLOW THROUGH

Remember that focus is strategy, and where your focus goes, your energy flows—then everything grows. Think of your obstacles, then focus your intention, energy and light through the various scopes: the microscope, telescope and kaleidoscope. Next, use Level TEN-acity to overcome those challenges.

1. **Telescope**: In 1985 when he was living in his car, actor and comedian Jim Carrey famously wrote himself a check for $10 million for "acting services rendered," to cash 10 years in the future. One decade later, he was issued a check for his work in the movie *Dumb and Dumber* in the amount of…$10 million. Write down a date 10 years from now. What's the *one thing* you'd like to focus your telescope on for that time?
2. **Microscope**: Zoom in on the goal to identify the most immediate obstacle or issue that, if removed, will create momentum towards your 10-year *one thing*. How can shifting your focus help you overcome that obstacle?
3. **Kaleidoscope**: Circle a date on the calendar 30 days from now and schedule a meeting with one of the most trusted, creative and innovative members of your circle. Sit them down and get their perspective on your 10-year *one thing*.

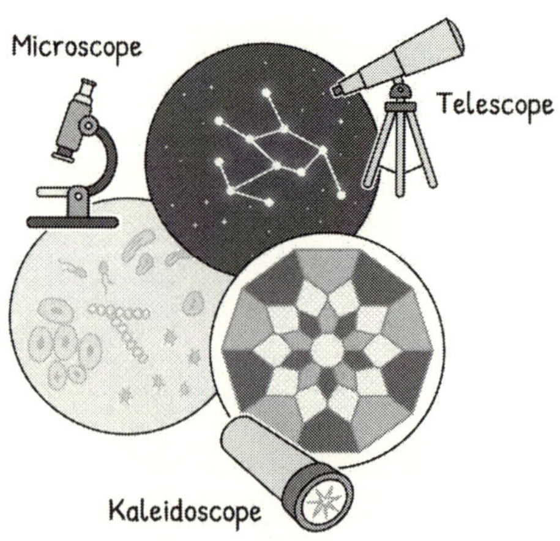


@Quoted Visually

# CHAPTER 6
# TENACITY$^2$

## DIRT, DEVELOPMENT + DEEDS

*"Getting strong is like moving a pile of dirt. Some days you use a shovel and some days you use a spoon, but what's important is you move some dirt."*
—John Welbourn

My Uncle Cool was Black Santa. I mean it—in appearance and in spirit. He was a giver and a servant to every person he met. He was a brick mason, and one of the most successful people in our family. When my bio dad was incarcerated when I was a year old, Uncle Cool stepped up and stepped in, helping Mom in every way he could and helping me when I needed a role model. He was a pillar she could lean on when her foundation was shaky. Unlike Santa, who pops up once a year, Uncle Cool was always there.

Uncle Cool gave me some great advice over the years about a lot of things, but it was his business advice that sowed the seeds of a lifetime of success. That advice—when nourished with tenacity—eventually grew and flourished into my legacy.

Like any young man, I became enamored with the flash of shiny new cars, and when it came time to buy my first, Uncle Cool told me, "Don't get wrapped up in these fancy cars yet. The time will come for that." So I bought a car that was about as old as me: a 1988 Honda Accord.

His most valuable and memorable advice echoed in my mind all through college. He told me, "When you get some money, put it in dirt. It's the one thing that nobody can make more of." Buying land became my first real investment strategy. When I was 18, I was working full time at Ben & Jerry's, and I had a couple thousand dollars saved in a CD that had earned a little interest. With those few extra dollars in my pocket, I asked myself, "Where can I buy some dirt?"

I bought small, distressed properties in very rural, country areas: foreclosures, short sales and tracts of land with timber that could be harvested, sold off and turned into lumber. I scoured available land in remote areas of Lee and Harnett Counties, tenaciously looking for properties that were under $10,000, and these became my entry into the real estate game. Because I was smart enough to know there was a lot I didn't know, I started researching. I attended seminars on real estate investing and learned how to be patient: dirt appreciates, but slowly. Most real estate investments are a long game. I also leaned on the Morehead-Cain network of professionals and business leaders to advise me on how to talk to bankers and build a relationship with a bank so that I could have the pieces in place when the time came for the big ask: a loan.

Back in 2008 when Eric and I were buying our first Ben & Jerry's franchise, funding for a risky and unsecured business loan was all but impossible. What we *did* have was a 12-acre tract of land that could serve as collateral and leverage for a smaller loan—the $50,000 line of credit that would help us to buy the first Chapel Hill store. There is value in asking for more, because it means if you only get some, it might just be enough. And as it turned out, we got exactly the right amount.

The property we used as collateral had a lot of timber that we eventually sold off for a little extra money, and then years later, we sold that property for much more than its original price to a family who wanted to build their dream home. Patience paid off. But the most beautiful lesson in all of this was that a pile of dirt was worth its weight in gold.

In the coming years, Eric and I would continue to buy short sales in distressed areas, and in 2010, we had enough to buy a handful of rental properties that gave us a little extra income every month. Katie and I dreamed of owning property in Chapel Hill so we could be closer to our primary business. It's a fairly affluent area though, and we knew we couldn't afford it yet. Instead, we purchased our first home *near* Chapel Hill. By then, we had just bought our second Ben & Jerry's franchise, and our savings were pretty much depleted. But we knew how to play the long game and were patient enough to wait a few years before investing again.

Around this time, one of our close friends, DP, came to us in crisis. He and his daughter, one of Nia's playmates, lived with his mom in a double-wide trailer on an acre-and-a-half of land in Chapel Hill. The property was going into foreclosure, and they were at risk of being homeless. These folks were like family to us, and we had to find a way to help them.

We dug deep into our savings, stretched our budget and were able to help them pay off their debt, get out of foreclosure and save the property. We made an arrangement with our friends that they could continue to live on the land rent-free for three years so they could rebuild and prepare for the future.

Being of service opens doors you can't always see at first. DP's mom was so grateful to us that she told us a 28-acre property in which she was a partial owner was also about to be foreclosed on. She said if we could handle the headache of sorting out the ownership puzzle, we could have her share.

I don't know if you have any experience with an "heirs property," but it's when a parcel is co-owned by multiple family members and passed down between generations without the involvement of local probate courts. Often there is no will, deed or formal estate strategy, so descendants inherit land without a clear title, and with every generation, more co-owners are added to the inheritance. Ownership percentages become family lore. "My great-uncle on my mom's side owned 11 percent, and it's now mine!" is hard to prove without documentation. Most heirs don't even bother to pay the taxes on their share but still want to claim it.

Enter The Honorable Judge Wade Barber. In 2014, I met Wade —a retired judge, district attorney-turned-estate-lawyer and a developer in his 70s. Retirement didn't suit Wade, and having just completed the development of an 8,000-acre property, he was looking for "interesting projects to keep his mind astute and engaged," as he put it. With his background in estate law and extra time on his hands, he was the perfect match to help me sort out the puzzle of the 28 acres of land and the generations of heirs attached to it.

Wade became a mentor to me, much in the same way Uncle Cool had been, and the work we did together untangling that knot of ownership was equivalent to earning a PhD in land law —and a valuable lesson in the importance of estate planning. It turned out that the 28 acres of land had 92 heirs attached—none of whom were paying taxes. Many of them were the great, great grandkids of second-marriage, step-sibling relations. While it's possible to "petition to partition" what you think is your portion of the land, it's only possible if you find all the owners and determine their percentage of ownership, as well as the value of that portion. It became a five-year passion project. We had dedicated ourselves to untying that knot.

In the cases where we were able to find the heirs and determine the worth of their percentage, we agreed to buy their portion—sometimes for as little as $500, depending on their relationship to the original share owner. Once we had bought up about 25 percent of the 28 acres, we placed an ad in the local paper to advise the remaining family members of our interest in purchasing. One by one, we made deals until we owned 92 percent of the property. That remaining eight percent was a real challenge, but I was tenacious. I took one more year and tracked down the remaining family members in New Jersey, eventually persuading them to sell over a few scoops of Chunky Monkey. I now owned 100 percent of the 28 acres in Chapel Hill. Finally, I owned a tangible asset of great value: I had a clean and clear deed to the property.

While doing all of our research, we learned that the adjacent 15-acre property was owned by a prominent and well-established local white family, the Coles. After generations spent establishing themselves as big land owners in Chapel Hill, the family had sold off nearly all of their North Carolina properties and relocated to Kentucky. When we tracked them down, we learned that they hadn't sold these last few acres because they were essentially worthless: they were land-locked with no road access. However, my shiny new 28 acres of land right next door *did* have road access. We were happy to take those last acres off their hands. Our persistence, patience and tenacity over the years delivered the deeds to over 50 acres of prime land in Chapel Hill. But more than that, we were acting in service to others—we were doing good deeds, and that had opened doors. Not only could we build a house now, we could build a compound on 50 acres.

My lawyer, mentor and newfound friend, Wade, was a firm believer in the value of dirt. Like me, he was a country boy who wanted some property in a great area. But he taught me that "dirt is just one of the 'Ds' in real estate." The second, which we'd already had some fun with, is *deeds*. And the third important "D" is *development*. He saw all that I was doing with Primo and Ben & Jerry's franchises, and he told me, "You're already a developer." Wade was a purposeful mentor, and he declared that in his lifetime of developing and investing, our project was the most meaningful use of his time because it inspired him at a key stage in his life.

I thought about how in the ice cream world, you buy ice cream wholesale in bulk, then sell it by the scoop at a retail price.

It's a big jump from ice cream scoops to subdivisions and real estate development, but Primo was built on thinking big. How could I take this tub of land and divide it into bite-sized scoops for houses?

In order to build a major mixed-use subdivision in my area, you need a minimum of 50 acres and highway access. My 50 acres now felt too small, and even though it had road access, it was too far from the highway to have true commercial/mixed-use appeal. Seeking advice, I connected with a good friend of mine, Andy. Andy was an experienced local developer, and his business partner Warren happened to own 35 acres on the highway adjacent to me. We decided to form a group, combine our holdings and acquire a few adjacent properties that brought us up to a 100-acre development project with highway access in Chapel Hill.

That call for help from my friend DP and my willingness to take on a risk and assist him led to me helping local Black families sort through their complicated land holdings, putting money in their pockets and eventually making me the owner of 28 acres of land. That initial parcel became 50 acres which ultimately grew to 100.

We eventually brought that 100 acres to its highest potential by creating a mixed-use, compact community with 203 single family homes, businesses, walkable streets, townhouses and affordable residences for low-income families. Everything worth investing in takes patience and time to develop. But you, too, can be a developer—by harvesting your own potential and fueling your work with a spirit of service and a healthy dose of tenacity.

## THERE'S FORTUNE IN THE FOLLOW THROUGH

What is the "dirt" in your life that you can till to develop it into something beyond your wildest dreams? Remember that being of service is the fertilizer that will enable you to harvest your full potential.

1. What are a couple of good deeds that you can focus on and pursue passionately in the years to come: literally in the form of real estate ownership and figuratively by making a huge impact on the life of someone who needs it?
2. Where in your life are you most tenacious?
3. Who is your Uncle Cool? Who are your mentors? (Hint: If you can't readily think of someone who functions as a mentor for you, find someone who has what you want and cultivate a relationship with them.)

# CHAPTER 7
# THE COMMUNI-KEYS
## COMMUNICATION + SELF-TALK

*"How do I listen to others as if everyone were my master speaking to me his cherished last words."*

—Hafiz

Top-notch communication is the lifeblood of businesses and entrepreneurs everywhere. *Inc. Magazine* recently published an article called "Poor Communication Is Costing You Money," detailing research about how employees with poor communication can impact the bottom line of every business. One report revealed that the global cost of poor business communication can cost around $12,000 per employee, per year, which is close to $40 billion annually. That same report says companies whose leaders have strong communication skills produce a 47 percent higher return over a five-year period.

What's the problem? The financial damage to companies can depend on a number of factors, including the severity of poor communication, the impact on others within the company, the business relationships with other enterprises and just how long it takes to resolve the problem. But the heart of the issue is that most people never receive any kind of communication training, so they lack the necessary skills.

Companies are made up of people, and every person has a different background and personality. Domineering people tend to overpower other voices and limit team engagement and company morale, which ultimately impairs team connectedness and therefore efficiency. These personalities can also lead to unhealthy working relationships loaded with unresolved conflict, and no one knows how to talk about it. That tension can lead to high turn-over rates due to poor morale.

When it comes to layoffs, companies that don't communicate effectively with their remaining staff are unknowingly creating a culture of fear and resentment. If people are afraid of being fired, they won't speak up when there is a problem, which contributes to the cycle of inefficiency and unhappiness that began with poor communication.

If you're a business owner, you can get ahead of these problems by investing in workplace communication training. These skill-building programs teach everything from confidence, self awareness and coping skills to impact, reporting and conflict defusion. But if you're just starting out as an entrepreneur, you can get ahead of the communication game by mastering what we at Primo call the "Seven Communi-KEYS to Success." To effectively apply these keys to life, you need to be curious and willing to look closely at the language you use (or as we call it, your "lexicon").

Between 2016 and 2018 when Primo was laser focused on scaling the business, we knew we had to grow our team. At the same time, our success as a company depended on our ability to cultivate our team so that they embodied the Primo values and acted as examples of our extraordinary legacy. We knew we needed a clear way to teach our vision in order to train top-tier staff. That's when we started to hone and refine our Communi-KEYS.

Before we jump in, let's first look at the word "communication." The first two letters, "co," mean "with, together or jointly." Think co-worker, co-producer, co-host, company, common. All of these words indicate that their meaning includes more than one person. I also like the word "commune," a group that lives together and shares responsibilities. Along those lines, the word "communicate" means the sharing and exchange of ideas and information. It implies being in contact with others, being in touch with their ideas and finding a common meeting place or common ground where ideas are freely exchanged.

Our seven Communi-KEYS are the best practices on effective and elevated communication. They'll not only help you *communicate* your thoughts and ideas more effectively, they'll also help you become a better listener.

## THE SEVEN COMMUNI-KEYS TO MASTERING COMMUNICATION

### COMMUNI-KEY 1: SELF-TALK

*"All conversations are with myself and sometimes they involve others."*
—Susan Scott, *Fierce Conversations*

If I could put this Communi-KEY in 3D neon letters with fireworks jumping off the page to get your attention, I would. Self-talk is all the stories we tell ourselves about ourselves. It is the master key for communication—the key that unlocks every door to success. In architecture, a keystone is a wedge-shaped stone that is placed at the top of an arch or vault to lock the other stones into place and enable the structure to support its weight. Self-talk is the keystone to dynamic and effective communication, and it keeps all valuable relationships secure. It is my most valuable self-development tool, and is the heartbeat of CEO Life.

The only person who lives in your mind is you, and your self-talk determines what kind of neighborhood your mind is. Is it dangerous, with insults and negative messages flying at you from every direction? Or is it a haven, where you go when you need reminders of how great your extraordinary life is? The Communi-KEY of self-talk is the way you communicate with yourself, and you can either build yourself from the inside out, or destroy yourself.

Psychologists and psychiatrists encourage people to talk to themselves. This is a self-soothing technique that is a very healthy form of self-care. Talking to yourself (in the car, in the shower or on a walk) can improve your mental health, reduce anxiety and depression, help you make the best decisions, increase your productivity and performance and help you regulate your emotions. I'm not a mental health professional, but I've learned that the most important conversation I can have is the one I have with myself.

Back in Chapter 5, I talked about how a series of business decisions led to me losing $100,000 in one year as well as a devastating lawsuit. My self-talk was as dark as it comes. Thoughts like *you're stupid, you're a failure, you're broke* were spinning around like a hurricane in my mind, and I was lost in that spiral. And the thing was, I *knew better.* I am a man of faith, and I know that my God would never abandon me. I had abandoned myself and was adrift in a dark sea of negativity. I was trapped in my mind and believing the self-limiting messages that I heard on repeat, and I was making bad assumptions about everything in my life.

But remember that shirt? My wife Katie gave me a T-shirt with the *ultimate* positive affirmation printed on it which shed some light on my mind and helped me see my way out of the darkness.

*The genius thing we did was we didn't give up.*

This became my mantra, my affirmation and my prayer. That was when I learned the value of daily affirmations. Not just when I feel bad, not just as a pick-me-up when I need a boost.

Repeating positive affirmations to myself is a daily commitment I make to nourish my spirit, my soul, my confidence and my mind.

---

## AFFIRMATIONS

Affirmations are positive statements that can help you shift out of negative thought patterns and promote positive thinking. You can use affirmations to challenge you, motivate you and replace negative talk and ideas with positive and uplifting thinking to help you reach your full potential every day. The more consistently you say your affirmations, the more your mind and heart begins to believe them. That belief will then be reflected in your actions, choices and decisions that affect you and others.

Every strong opinion or thought we have is profoundly influenced by our past experiences, which affect our interpretation of the world around us. But we can't let our past negative experiences determine our present or our hopes for the future—our goals and aspirations. Affirmations help us reframe those negative experiences into lessons and events that happened *for us* not *to us.*

Another great thing about affirmations is that they improve our emotional intelligence, which then increases and enhances our communication skills. Emotional intelligence is a valuable social skill that enables us to manage, understand and express our feelings. Affirmations boost our confidence, determination, empathy and self awareness, shaping our self-talk into a powerful driving force towards success and CEO Life. You cannot lead and inspire others if you yourself are not inspired.

You can write out affirmations in a journal, put them on post-it notes around the house, frame them on your wall, repeat them to yourself or even subscribe to an app that sends them to you throughout the day. (I like the app I Am, which nudges me with positivity every two hours. I like to take a screenshot of my favorites and re-read them or share them with others.)

A good affirmation is:

- **In the present tense**: "I am confident" is better than "I want to be more confident."
- **Specific**: "I am prepared and excited for today's presentation" instead of "I'll do a good job today."
- **Descriptive**: "I am the perfect fit for this position" versus "I want a job."
- **Phrased with realistic expectations**: "I'm healing more every day" is a better way of saying "I'm over this."

At the end of this chapter, I've included some of my favorite affirmations, and I hope they inspire you.

## SAVERS

Back in Chapter 2, I introduced the SAVERS technique that I learned in Outward Bound. It was so life-changing that I'm repeating it here. Remember: you can use this method daily, or when you're going through a particular crisis and you need a lifeline.

## MUSIC

Everything in this world is made of vibrations. The desk in front of me is made of molecules vibrating against each other; the cells in our bodies are vibrating. Every noise we hear is a vibration. We all know people with "good vibes"—they operate at a high frequency that radiates positivity. We also know some folks with "bad vibes"—they bring us down and make us feel worse about the world.

I think the fastest way to change the vibrations in a room or in my head is with music. I listen to music first thing in the morning, while I'm at work, while I exercise, in the car between meetings, on the plane, in the evening when I'm with my family—I've got music going all the time. I have a playlist of songs that make me feel better, without fail, every time I listen to them. You can make a playlist for every mood you might be in throughout the day, and one for every mood you *want* to be in.

Music can be a time machine, taking you back to that high school party, the first dance at your wedding, Saturday mornings in the car with Mom or the day your kid was born. I challenge you to incorporate music into your daily life and see how it improves your mood and your self-talk. Listen to something new. Let it take you somewhere.

## GUIDED MEDITATION

I've heard it said that praying is talking to God and meditation is listening to God. All you have to do to meditate is find some silence inside yourself. You can meditate in a park, in your car, in your office, on a walk or in a crowded subway. You can do it for one minute or an hour. All you need is some uninterrupted time to guide your thoughts and tap into your subconscious.

Some people struggle with sitting still for even a minute. If you're one of those people, I want you to challenge yourself to start with 60 seconds, then over the course of a few weeks, work your way up to 15 minutes. Before long it will feel like a natural state of stillness that you crave. If the sound of your thoughts tend to be screams, then you might enjoy a guided meditation. If you go to YouTube, you can plug in any word next to meditation and find videos from three minutes to eight hours that talk you through the process. You can even find 12-hour sleep meditations that help you release anxiety and fear throughout the night.

There are also some great apps for meditation. Breathe is my favorite. There are specialized sessions for anxiety, creativity, insomnia, visualization and depression—you name it. Some others are Headspace, 10 Percent and Calm.

Sometimes just being in silence is all you need, or being outside in nature. As your meditation practice advances, you might consider attending a meditation retreat. These are organized all over the world and probably in your own town. They can be a day trip or a 30-day silent retreat—it depends on your life, business and career needs, but these time-outs can provide much-needed clarity to improve your self-talk, making you a better listener, leader and communicator.

## DAILY ROUTINE

My self-talk completely depends on how committed I am to my daily routine, beginning with when I first open my eyes. When I wake up, I'm very careful not to look at my phone, check my emails or respond to text messages until I have my mind ready for outside influences.

- I have a glass of water.
- I step outside for some fresh air (and hopefully some sunshine).
- I stretch quickly with my music playing.

- I go to my meditation room.
- I read a daily devotional.
- I journal each morning.
- I write three "appreciations"—three things, no matter how big or how small, that I really appreciate: *I appreciate a great night's sleep. I appreciate the breeze outside, the sunflowers blooming. I appreciate the awesome team that I work with.*
- I write down my three priorities for that day—what three things, if done, will make me feel fulfilled? *Eating properly, having a great manager training session and making it to my daughter's school for lunch.*

Once I've completed all of these steps in my routine, I am ready to be that ultimate communicator and leader for my team. *Now* I can dive into the text messages, emails and calls—and I'm ready for anything.

I also have a night routine.

- I write down my three amazements: What three things from the day truly amazed me? *I'm amazed at how well my flight to Atlanta went. I am amazed at my team's self-sufficiency. I'm amazed at how dope the crowd was in Raleigh tonight and how much energy they brought to the session.*
- I listen to a guided meditation: Sometimes I will choose a body scan that releases tension in certain areas of my body. Sometimes I choose to invoke messages about communication, gratitude or anxiety.

Adopting these tools will help you prioritize and perfect positive self-talk, which will improve your mental health, increase your confidence, help you feel empowered and contribute to your vitality and general happiness. Those qualities, in turn, will make you approachable, teachable and emotionally intelligent, which will make you an effective and expert communicator.

## COMMUNI-KEY 2: ATTENTIVE LISTENING AND DEEP PONDERING

Communication is not simply talking. In fact, at Primo we understand that the most respectful communication has nothing to do with talking. There are two imperatives to respectful communication: attentive listening and deep pondering.

Attentive listening means that rather than impatiently waiting for the person speaking to end their comments so that you can jump into your response, you actively listen, focus and concentrate on the speaker and what they're saying, meaning and implying. To truly understand what is being said, you have to be a detective. There are the spoken words, then there are the meanings behind the words. There's the intent or purpose of what's being said, and there's an implied meaning behind those words. As a detective, you're looking for clues to the best way you can respond.

Listening intently allows you to learn the other person's story. You don't want to be the kind of person who is thinking *what's in it for me?* And you don't want to assume you know what is being said or asked for. Move from certainty to curiosity.

Once you've intently listened to the other person, you need to take a moment to deeply ponder what's been said. Notice I say "ponder" instead of "think." When I hear the word "ponder" it sounds to me like a pond, or a deep well where the ideas and words can swim around for a bit until I dip in and catch one. I'm letting everything sink in. It's my job to absorb all that is being given and to respectfully consider it. This means being people-centered and considerate of the other person's needs, wants and work.

Sometimes your secret weapon is silence. This doesn't come

naturally to most of us, so know that the more you do it, the more natural it will feel. I've noticed that intently listening isn't something that people in Western culture do particularly well, and we seem pretty judgmental as a result. Eastern cultures with a historical tradition of mindfulness seem to listen better, and they aren't in as much of a hurry to respond or interject.

While you ponder the other person's intention and needs, consider what their "higher" meaning might be, as well as their "deeper" meaning. Higher meaning implies that there's a bigger picture, while deeper meaning includes all of the signals they're implicitly sending.

After some time pondering what has been communicated, you'll find that clarifying questions come up in your mind, as well as alternative thoughts. Those clarifying questions can then be translated into *quality questions.* The quality of your questions is directly connected to your quality of life.

If you want to develop your listening skills, check out the books below as resources:

- *How to Listen* by Thich Nhat Hanh
- *How to Listen with Intention: The Foundation of True Connection, Communication and Relationships* by Patrick King
- *The Power of Listening: How to Improve Relationships by Becoming an Active Listener* by Damian Blair

## COMMUNI-KEY 3: CLEAR, CONCRETE AND CONCISE COMMUNICATION

The attention span of most people has grown shorter over the past two decades. Technology is partly the reason. The remote control for our televisions, the delete key on our laptops and the scroll function on social media have turned us into people who are quick to shift our attention away from that which doesn't immediately catch our eye. Practicing clear, concrete, concise communication allows us to get our point across quickly and efficiently, before we lose the other person's attention.

The CEO who uses clear, concrete and concise communication is going to be heard and understood. Two particular techniques come to mind: teachers and preachers.

Teachers use a "sandwich" approach to communication which has three main steps:

1) Tell them what I'm going to tell them
2) Tell them
3) Summarize what I told them

Think about high school or college courses. At the beginning of a quarter you get a course syllabus: an outline of everything the teacher is going to focus on throughout the class. At the end, they wrap the course up with a study guide, and you take a test or turn in a project that proves that you were listening.

On any given day, the lecture could begin with, "Today we're going to review." The teacher talks about the subject for an hour, then ends by either saying, "Thank you for your attention as I talked about…" or by tricking you with, "Tomorrow we'll further discuss this topic."

This is an effective way to communicate because it organizes the teacher's intentions in three easy-to-follow steps. You walk away with your notes and a reading assignment that further solidifies the lesson, and hopefully you've absorbed everything. The test will determine that.

Preachers, on the other hand, communicate a little differently. They often introduce a subject and then say, "I have five points I want to share with you this morning." By laying out those talking points ahead of time, they have created a contract with the people in the congregation who are now prepared to listen for those five points. Effective preachers will label each point as they reach it, so the listeners can keep their bearings: "Now, on to point number four..." Preachers know they can lose their audience if they abandon the contract and keep on talking beyond the promised points.

You always want to match your communication style to your audience, because it helps them feel respected and remain engaged. Are you presenting to a group of high school kids on their way to college? Is it a room of CEOs? Maybe it's a staff meeting with a mix of folks in their 20s and 30s. Whatever style you use to communicate, the information must be accessible, relevant and digestible.

## COMMUNI-KEY 4: MASTER THE TRIFECTA OF VERBAL, NON-VERBAL AND WRITTEN COMMUNICATION

There are three main types of communication, and to be a successful business owner and leader you have to learn how to be effective with all three: verbal, non-verbal and written. You might have a particular skill set where one of these comes easier for you than another, but all three are opportunities to connect with people and convey information. As you develop your leader skill set, be certain you're mastering all three.

### VERBAL

Most great leaders understand the power of voice. Speaking with a grounded, confident and resonant voice makes you a captivating presenter. Most successful politicians have learned this skill, regardless of the message they're delivering. Actors on stage learn voice technique so they can capture and maintain their audience's attention for long stretches of time. Coaches and public speakers practice their presentations in front of a camera so they can catch and correct moments of weakness or lapses in confidence when they might lose the attention of their listeners. How you speak can be as important as what you're saying.

Having a broad vocabulary is useful because it gives us more ways to express ourselves. Especially when we're nervous, we might overuse words or phrases like, "generally," "actually," or "you know what I mean." Used sparingly, these are fine. But when they're scattered in every other sentence, they can be distracting and dilute our message.

There are a lot of ways to expand your vocabulary, one of which is reading. Regardless of whether you're reading (books, articles, magazines or a newspaper), you're going to learn something new. If you come across a word you don't know, look it up. If you're old school, use a dictionary. If you're more digital, plug it into Google. Look for synonyms: other words that are similar to or mean the same thing as that word.

Some people push back on reading: they think it's hard to focus or it's a waste of time. Some people even have learning disorders that make it challenging to concentrate when they read. I have a secret: audiobooks count as reading. If you're listening to a book, a podcast or choosing to use your phone's reader app, it counts! You're learning new information and you're growing your vocabulary.

Writing is another way to build your vocabulary. When you're writing down your thoughts and ideas, you need to find new ways to express yourself. Let's say it's a journal entry—something very low stakes, as no one else will be reading what you write. However, it's an opportunity for you to practice new ways of expression.

If you write, "I'm sad today," elaborate on that idea—explain what you mean by sad. Are you in mourning? Are you depressed? Are you feeling compassion for someone else? The more you write, the more confident you will get with new ways of using your expanding vocabulary.

There are also word games and apps that can help you learn new words and build your word arsenal. Scrabble or Words with Friends are games that will expose you to new vocabulary. If you're playing Scrabble and the only letter you have is "Z," how many words can you build with that one, uncommon letter? Try downloading an app that gives you a new word each day so you can challenge yourself to use it in a sentence with every conversation you have.

There are daily opportunities to find new ways to express yourself. Let's say you're in a meeting, two of your staff members just gave a presentation, and you want more information. Since the goal is communication, how can you phrase your request? You could say, "Let's dissect your presentation," but that choice of words could put your staff on the defensive; they worked hard on their project, and now their boss is going to break it down and break *them* down?

Instead, try saying, "That was interesting. Tell me more." This welcoming, curious approach both respects the information that is there and encourages a deeper dive into the details that may be missing. Your vocabulary and ability to phrase things in a creative way will help you master the art of communication and transform your leadership.

## NON-VERBAL

In every interaction, we are telling people something with our body language. This is non-verbal communication. If you pay attention you'll notice how people are standing and what messages or cues they are unintentionally sending to reveal their true feelings.

You can have an entire, nonverbal conversation using just body language. If you're having an exchange with someone who speaks another language, you can pantomime, gesture with your hands, point with your fingers and use facial expressions to get your ideas across.

Imagine you've stopped for directions while driving from one town to another, but you don't speak the language. You might use your hands to mime driving, your shoulders and arms to ask for directions, your eyes to intimate confusion and maybe your whole body to turn around in circles and show that you're lost. Next thing you know, the stranger you've stopped might be gesturing with one arm to show which way you should go, holding up two fingers to tell you how many turns you should take, and you'll both give each other the thumbs up to say, "Okay! Thank you!"

There are different ways we use our body language to communicate non-verbally with others, and with all our physical expressions to choose from, we can either invite conversation and a pleasant exchange, or we can bring an interaction to a full stop.

**Types of Expression**

| TYPES OF EXPRESSION | POSITIVE AND ENGAGED: ENTHUSIASTICALLY INVITING COMMUNICATION | NEGATIVE, DISMISSIVE, AGGRESSIVE AND CLOSED OFF |
|---|---|---|
| Touch | Holding a handshake firmly while making eye contact; light touch on arm or shoulder (depending on how well you know the person). | Weak handshakes, using arms as a barrier. |
| Space | Allowing personal space (one and half to four feet); intimate space for close friends and family is six to 18 inches. | Standing too far away indicates disinterest. |
| Eye Contact | Direct eye contact; following their body language to indicate understanding; raised eyebrows. | Breaking eye contact and looking elsewhere, checking your phone or watch, furrowed brows. |
| Gestures | Sitting up straight; open posture, relaxed hands and arms; thumbs up; touching the heart: open hand gestures. | Wide arms to appear larger; hands on hips; fidgeting or tapping fingers. |
| Body Movement | Note taking, nodding, tilting the head; leaning into the conversation or towards someone. | Turned away from the other person; leg jiggling or foot tapping; shifting from foot to foot. |
| Postures | Open, relaxed arms. | Folded arms, crossed legs away from the other person; using hands to shield eyes or mouth. |

## WRITTEN

I mentioned earlier how writing can help improve your vocabulary and communication skills. Writing in a journal or jotting down notes to yourself doesn't have any impact on others and is a safe way to build skills. But for a lot of people, there is nothing more daunting than having to share thoughts, directives or plans in writing. Even writing an email can be anxiety-inducing, especially if they're trying to attract business or close a deal.

Then there's writing for public speaking. Whether it's a

PowerPoint slide deck for a work meeting, a presentation for clients or a speech for a room full of colleagues, writing out and condensing ideas onto a couple of note cards and then speaking in front of other people is intimidating. It can make even the most confident person feel vulnerable.

One crucial thing you can do to improve as a writer is read. Read those ads and e-blast marketing emails to learn about industry standards of communication. What do you like about what you read? How is your business different? Read articles and how-to books. Read inspirational quotes and sermons. Read rejection letters. Everything you read will improve your writing.

Mastering your writing skills will improve every area of communication and elevate your leadership in every area of your life and business. Expressing your feelings in a letter to a loved one, preparing marketing and promotional materials, responding to a high-stakes email or even posting on social media all require flawless writing skills. Here are some of the ways your communication will improve when you master the written word:

- Your ability to collaborate effectively will improve
- You will tactfully navigate challenging conversations
- You will provide constructive and thoughtful feedback
- Your confidence as a public speaker will grow
- You will deepen your relationships with others
- You will develop your career and build your business

Beyond reading, there are a number of techniques you can use to develop your writing skill. I recommend you practice them daily, but especially when you're working on something that demands clarity and concise delivery. Writers use methods like these when they're trying to get some traction for their ideas, whether it's for a book, a movie or an article. You can try these before sending an email or when you've got a great business idea to sell to your partners.

## MIND MAPPING

Mind mapping is a brainstorming technique you can use to organize your ideas. When you're done, you'll have a flow chart showing how your brain works: how one thought or idea is connected to another, and how they're all interrelated. It's a great way to map your free-flowing thoughts and inspiration.

On a sheet of paper or a blank computer screen, place a word that is at the heart of your message, problem or main topic. For example, if you're planning a management seminar, you might put "LEADERSHIP" in the middle of the page and circle it. That's your central subject.

Now, draw arrows from the word, brainstorm what comes to mind when you think of leadership, and connect each of those thoughts or words to the arrows. You might write down concepts like "culture," "performance," "relationships" and "training." Those are your main associations with your central theme.

Now draw arrows, lines or branches off those words, and add more associations with those ideas. Suddenly, you have a page or screen full of keywords to use for crafting your message.

This technique works for individuals and for groups. That means you can do it on your own during a deep focus session or in the meeting to capture all the brilliant ideas flowing from your team. You can try this on a whiteboard for everyone to contribute, or you can take five or ten minutes and ask each attendee to brainstorm on their own.

## BULLET POINTS

Long documents full of dense text are not welcomed and often go unread. Even long emails with blocks of text are frequently ignored. In this era of emojis and character limits, most people just don't have the time or attention span to stay tuned to your stream of consciousness—they get mad when a commercial interrupts their favorite show! If you can't communicate in a way that keeps your readers' attention, they're going to press "skip" on the whole thing.

When communicating ideas in writing—whether it's a text, email, letter or PowerPoint presentation, effective writers use "skinny paragraphs" with just two or three sentences, followed by bullet points to communicate their message. White space calms the reader. Breaking up your ideas with text boxes, graphics and colors is also appealing. Discipline yourself by writing out focused, concise ideas, then add images to deepen understanding or inspirational quotes to punctuate your message. All of these techniques keep the reader's attention and interest.

## COMMUNI-KEY 5: STORYTELLING

Early in our lives, we learned from the stories we were told. When our parents, preachers, teachers or librarians read to us, those books captured our imaginations and helped us make sense of the world around us.

The beautiful thing is, we never grow out of that childhood love for well-told stories: they connect us to each other and to the past. Stories bridge gaps between generations, social groups, religions and cultures. They create communion and community, stimulate our emotions, imagination and our senses. A well-told tale delivers a message and leaves an impact that can last a lifetime.

To CEO Life, being an effective storyteller is a superpower. It's a way to verbally illustrate an idea or experience while engaging your listener, helping them feel connected to your message. It humanizes you and displays your authenticity. Great leaders know that storytelling enhances communication: it helps them craft a narrative around their message that makes it even more understandable and impactful.

A compelling story has a vivid setting, an enticing plot,

dynamic characters and a memorable message. Use descriptive language that evokes a sensory response—what did the setting smell like? What was the main character feeling? Make sure there's a beginning, middle and an end, and think in terms of setup, confrontation and resolution. There's always a problem or a challenge that has to be resolved, so make sure your conclusion is satisfying and clarifying. You want your audience to say, "Aha! That's how this story is connected to the central idea of this presentation!" Like a gymnast, you have to "stick the landing," so by the end of the story, the message should be obvious.

Make sure that you tell your story with energy and passion—those are the traits of a remarkable communicator. Think of yourself telling your story around a campfire: the more committed you are to delivering a captivating performance, the more memorable you and your message will be.

## COMMUNI-KEY 6: ANALOGIES

A straightforward directive is not always the fastest way to communicate a complicated or complex idea. Sometimes, sharing an example outside of the business context can better drive home a point, and using analogies can help bridge the understanding gap. Analogies are great for illustrating an unfamiliar concept: by drawing the connection for your audience, you can help them understand.

Analogies connect two ideas by comparing one thing to another. Sports may have nothing to do with finance, but if we're talking about a financial goal, it's easy to understand "reaching the goal post" as an analogy for a successful accomplishment. Similarly, if you're talking about how every team member contributes their own unique, valuable experience to complete a project, you can say, "Each voice is an important contribution to the choir, and many individuals singing together can create a powerful harmony."

Here are a few more examples:

- A "self-check" in basketball is when players are so afraid of failure that they never shoot the ball. You can use this to encourage team members to try new ideas without worrying about the result.
- Calling for a "mulligan," or a do-over in golf is like testing new software and having to start over with new code.
- Master chefs pivoting from a soufflé to an omelet when they run out of key ingredients can be compared to simplifying a task so it gets done instead of endlessly laboring toward perfection.

## COMMUNI-KEY 7: WORD CHOICE, LANGUAGE AND PHRASEOLOGY

The language you use to communicate your ideas can influence the impression you leave on your customer, client or employee. Your communication will have more impact on the listener or reader if you appropriately use powerful and evocative words.

Having a rich vocabulary demonstrates your eloquence, sophistication and intellect. Using the right words in the right context—whether it's written or spoken communication—will establish you as an authority on any subject.

I like to organize words into two categories: Rotten Words and Super Words. Rotten Words are overused, sometimes crass and at best, unimaginative. Super Words evoke an emotion and stimulate curiosity. They prove you are thoughtful and have original ideas. Rotten Words are predictable, obvious and uninteresting. Super Words are clever and inventive. There are also Rotten Phrases: sayings that are mundane and cliché. They are so uninspired, they should be retired forever.

Work on building an arsenal of Super Words and Super Phrases to make your message more engaging to your audience. Here are some examples of word substitutions to consider:

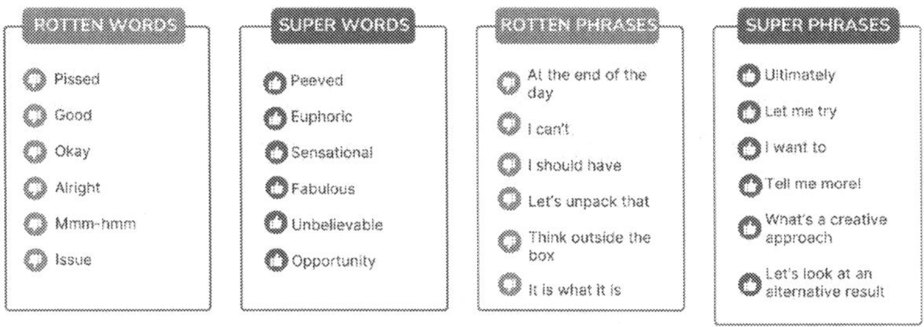


In that first example, "pissed" versus "peeved," even if you are upset that your staff was late to the meeting, saying that you're "peeved" is more humorous and disarming. If you say, "You've pissed me off," you're probably going to get a defensive response. If you say, "I'm peeved!" you're still communicating that you're annoyed, but you're more likely to be met with light-hearted apologies.

## THERE'S FORTUNE IN THE FOLLOW THROUGH

1. Which of the Seven Communi-KEYS do you excel at and rely on the most? What's one thing you can do to use that Communi-KEY in service to others?
2. Which Communi-KEY would you like to get better at?
3. Map out your daily routine to include affirmations that can improve your self-talk. One that I have used since I was a young athlete is from Heartsill Wilson:

*This is the beginning of a new day. God has given me this day to use as I will. I can waste it or use it for good. But what I do today is important because I'm exchanging a day of my life for it. When tomorrow comes, this day will be gone forever, leaving in its place that which I have traded. I want it to be gain not loss, good not evil, success not failure. I know I shall not regret the price I have paid for it because the future is just a whole string of nows!*

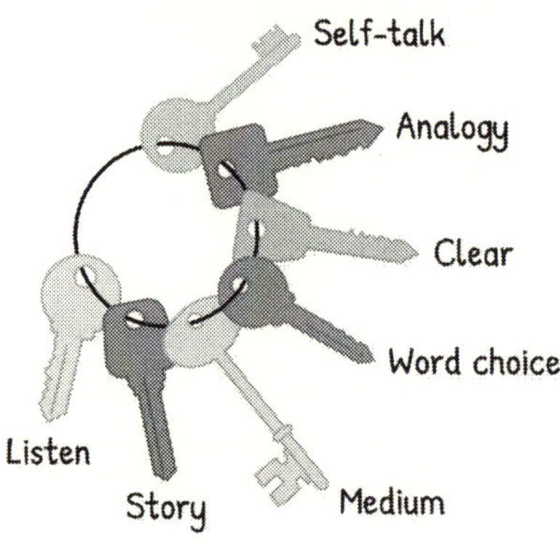

# PART III: LIFE

*Noun*:

Old English līf, of Germanic origin; related to Dutch lijf, German leib, 'body"; also to live.

1. The condition that distinguishes animals and plants from inorganic matter, including the capacity for growth, reproduction, functional activity and continual change preceding death.
2. Either of the two states of a person's existence, separated by death.
3. The period between the birth and death of a living thing, especially a human being.
4. Vitality, vigor or energy.

# CHAPTER 8
# LEARNING BOSS TIME FROM A KINDERGARTENER

## TIME MANAGEMENT + TIME MASTERY

*"The butterfly counts not months but moments, and has time enough."*
—Rabindranath Tagore

Family is everything. I would have nothing in this life if I didn't have my family. Growing up, every advantage I had was because of the support of my Memaw and my mom. Today, I only succeed because of the love and understanding of my wife, Katie. And there is nothing more buoyant than the joy I receive when I spend quality time with my kids.

There's nothing that forces you to see the passage of time in fast-forward like watching your kids grow up, and my business has grown up in tandem with my kids. Nia, my daughter, was born in 2010, 20 months after I bought my first Ben & Jerry's franchise. My son Nox was born in 2015, while I was taking the first steps to scale my business and integrate a second store. But Katie has been there from the beginning—she helped me pour the concrete for the foundation of our CEO Life.

As a couple of childhood athletes, it's fitting that we met on the court. We were in middle school, and there I was on the way to a game in my suit and tie (Coach was a traditionalist). Katie was in the middle of a game, playing point guard. The ball went out of bounds, and she chased it right past me. Stud that I was in middle school, I winked at her—of course.

We went to the same high school in Goldston, North Carolina. Interracial relationships aren't easy in the rural South, but we managed to keep in touch with AOL Instant Messenger (if you're old enough to remember that). Then we maintained a friendship through college, which eventually brought us together by the time I was in my last year at UNC, Chapel Hill. Next came Ben & Jerry's and Primo, followed by Nia's birth.

Those early years of family and business building are a blur of road trips, Katie and Nia riding along as my most trusted sidekicks. Because Nia was the only grandchild in both of our families, we also had a lot of family support: my in-laws had the time and we had the need. Our enterprise kept growing, so in 2015 when Nox was born, I faced a lot of new challenges as a business owner. By then, the grandparents were splitting their time among a brood of grandkids, and with my hectic schedule, I struggled to find balance—there never seemed to be enough time.

I had always looked at time differently from the folks around me. Even back when I was in college, most kids lived in the dorms and loved feeling free and grown up. Not me: I used my scholarship benefits to map out my school career in a unique way.

I saw that Memaw, now in her 70s, was going to have to cover all the heavy chores that I had been doing—and that didn't sit right with me. Memaw was my biggest cheerleader and advocate, and I couldn't abandon her. I had the job at Ben & Jerry's, but I faced a problem: How was I going to go to school full time, work and live at home so I could take care of Memaw? In response, I got creative with time mastery.

Memaw's house was just 45 minutes from school. Instead of living on campus, I decided to live at home and commute to school, so instead of paying for housing and a meal card with my scholarship money, I could put those funds toward taking care of my family. I got the house set up with plumbing and running water, and bought Memaw a new bed for $600. We were living like royalty.

This was also when I first discovered the advantages of block scheduling. I set up my class schedule so that all of my classes were on Tuesdays and Thursdays. That gave me Mondays, Wednesdays and Fridays off. Block scheduling gave me flexibility and the ability to earn income on those off days. Wednesdays were my homework days. I became a master of my time.

Because I wasn't in school all day every day, I had more availability for work, and I quickly earned a reputation at Ben & Jerry's for being a valuable employee. Also, since I was mobile and commuting, I could visit the Raleigh and Durham stores. I went quickly from a minimum-wage scooper to a shift leader, then to an area leader.

This early lesson in the value of owning my time set me on a course for success. But being a single college student is very different from being a husband, a father and a business owner who is pulled in a million directions from one moment to the next.

In 2015, I was 29, my business was flourishing and my family was growing with the addition of Nox. Along with that personal growth came an increase in my entrepreneurial responsibilities. I wore a lot of hats: payroll, scheduling, scooping and customer care, marketing and building sales all while developing partnerships and cultivating relationships.

Our daughter Nia was now in school, so we couldn't just put the kids in their car seats and hit the road together like we could before the whirlwind of school activities, sports, PTA duties and parent-teacher meetings. Part of growing a family means being flexible—and with baby Nox, we were experiencing the joys of a newborn who needs a parent every second of every day. I was also feeling helpless, watching the light of my life, Katie, struggle with postpartum depression. Some people call it the "baby blues," but that makes it sound cutesy and unserious. When someone you love doesn't feel like herself and has fluctuating hormones controlling her moods, you really learn just how powerless you are.

Mental health challenges are a whirlwind, an aspect of life we all face ourselves, either first or second hand. Katie is a part of me, and everything in my life was shifting because she needed my support in a new way. She had been a light for me during my dark night of the soul when I was facing lawsuits and fearing the worst. The idea of leaving her alone to handle all the parenting responsibilities while she was trying to keep her head above water was out of the question. Something had to give.

Then the *Triangle Business Journal* recognized me as a "Top 40 Under 40," up-and-coming business leader. The timing couldn't have been more auspicious: the award came with a scholarship to attend the John Grinnell Executive Leadership training program, and it was a game changer.

That week-long course in Wilmington, North Carolina was a total system upgrade that focused on self-improvement, bringing me back to my original entrepreneurial vision and my first sparks of inspiration. With the advantage of 360-degree feedback, it allowed me to see the blindspots in my business leadership. It taught me how to delegate and be less of a perfectionist. It was the reboot I needed.

I came back from those workshops a changed man, and I put what I learned into transforming Primo. As an immediate solution to my time-management problems, I promoted my accomplished friend Phillip Scotton to partner and full time Chief Operations Officer. With a strong COO running the background side of the business, I could now focus on being the CEO. Those changes gave me the best and most valuable gift of all: time.

But I still need reminders. Years later when my son Nox was in kindergarten, we had a routine at pick up. He and I would go to Chik-fil-A for an after-school snack. He was always hangry after school, but this ritual wasn't just about the food, it was about the time I was giving him. The reward after his long day was Daddy Time—that, and some delicious chicken.

One afternoon, I needed to pick up a friend at the airport about five minutes away, so I told Nox we'd go to Chik-fil-A first, then on to get my friend. Well, as I was turning into the drive-through, I got a call that there was a mix-up, and my friend had actually flown into a different airport that was two hours away. Apologizing to Nox, I said, "We'll get Chik-fil-A after we go to the airport." When he rightfully asked how long that would be, I said, "About two hours."

From the back seat, I heard a tiny, rage-filled voice yell, *"TWO HOURS!? THAT'S FOREVER! DO WE HAVE A GAZILLION JILLION HOURS TO LIVE!?"*

That perspective really helped me to change the way I think of two hours of time, and how it isn't necessarily linear. To me, two hours was 120 minutes. To Nox, it was an eternity. And because we don't live forever, we have to value every minute and every hour.

*"But do not forget this one thing, dear friends: With the Lord a day is like a thousand years, and a thousand years are like a day."*
*—2 Peter 3:8*

Time is a gift, and it's up to us to own and shape it so we can draw out every advantage. We have to become bosses of our time, or as I call it, "Boss Time." It's one of my seven principles to CEO Life. Boss Time is the art and science of creating a legacy by mastering time so that moments become meaningful memories. Remember, *you* are in charge of your time, and you can harness it so that every moment is purposeful and valued.

Here are some guidelines on how to apply the Boss Time principle to your life so that you get the most out of every moment.

## BENDING TIME

Physicists know that time is a mental concept. In her article, "Mastering the Art of Time Bending: Unlocking the Secrets of Your Reality," Dr. Kat Peoples challenges us to pay attention to all aspects of time so we can shape it to meet our needs. We humans created the concept of linear time so we could measure a sequence of events, one after the next. A schedule is really just a way to organize moments on a map, and the map happens to be a never-ending line.

But what if we took away that linear concept altogether? What if we erased the line and changed our perception? If we do this, we can have control over how fast or slow time passes. I think the most accessible way to change how we perceive time is to meditate.

We've all experienced those feelings of time standing still or time flying. When we meditate, we lose our marker for the passage of time. This altered state of consciousness helps us release our life-long concept of time. We can enter another dimension or even time travel! If we focus with intention on a specific memory, recalling everything we see, hear, taste, feel and smell, we are no longer in our living room—we're back on that beach on our honeymoon.

We can even use the power of intention to time travel to the future, where all of our energy is focused on imagining the results we wish to achieve. Where are we? What are we wearing? What do we see, hear or smell? When we use a kaleidoscopic focus on our intention, with our thoughts, energy and desire all moving towards achieving that result, we are no longer sitting at our desk—we're in the future, enjoying the fruits of today's choices and actions.

When we shed the concept of linear time, we are engrossed in the moment and our productivity increases. We are controlling the flow, and our creativity is unbound. As a result, we have sharper clarity, improved emotional states and stronger relationships because the time spent with the people we care about is intentional and focused—not measured on a linear map.

You can read Dr. Peoples' article at philosophicalhealing.com, and learn more about her techniques for mastering the art of time bending.

## LEAD AND MANAGE IN THREE TIME ZONES

Time zones aren't just the imaginary lines you cross when you fly across the country or around the globe. Time zones are the past, the future and the present. There are also cultural time zones. To CEO Life, you have to learn to master, lead and manage across all these time zones.

The effective executive is always scanning the landscape, analyzing data, evaluating situations and studying people. From one moment to the next, you are reviewing your options and making choices, executing decisions that will have an impact on your future. To make the right decisions, you require a telescopic focus on the future, the long-term timing of a strategist and the real-time discipline of a tactician.

Time slows down when you think long term—for example, in terms of decades. It's very common for folks to overplan what is possible inside of a year. But at the same time, we often underplan what's possible inside a decade.

Think back to a decade ago. What has changed? What have you accomplished? I know that for me, depending on the decade I review, my two children didn't exist. Now think ahead to 10 years into the future. If you're centered on the things around you in the moment and the things that are important to you today, you will value them even more when you imagine what they look like 10 years from now. It's easy to see what's important to you today, but what do you think will be important in the future? If you have a toddler, a lot will change in 10 years. What do tweens and teenagers like and need? If you are a new business owner working from home, will you have an office 10 years from now? Employees? Where will your office be? What will office culture look like?

In February of 2020, I was heavily focused on team and leadership development, knowing that the company I imagined in the future would be led and shaped by those people. I was living in the moment and looking towards that future, cultivating all the seeds we were planting when the pandemic hit. Ten years before that, I could not have imagined the impact of a global pandemic on my business or family. But today, I can look back at 2020 as a year of enormous growth for my company, despite those road blocks I couldn't predict at the time: restaurants closing, people not leaving their homes and people losing family members every day. Luckily, with empty stores and off-site event catering at a stand-still, Primo was in a position to pivot our focus to leadership development.

We mapped out our goals through the telescopic lens, and despite the business landscape in 2020 and 2021, Primo now has stores in the double-digits. With that hindsight, I can learn from the past as I look towards the future: how might a global pandemic affect my plans in the future? How will any kind of unpredictable event outside my control impact my business? What seeds can I plant today, with microscopic focus, that will help my business flourish down the line? We need to try to remain firmly in the present while learning from the past—and thinking in terms of how that past can predict the future.

Now for literal time zones. If I'm on Eastern Standard Time and my colleagues are on Pacific Standard Time, I need to be sensitive to where they are in their day. A 9 am call for me is great, because it's the kickoff to my morning and I'm ready to start checking things off my list. But it's only 6 am for my co-workers. Why did I schedule this call at a time when they haven't even had their coffee yet?

I can also use these different time zones to my advantage, so that if it's 3 pm for me, it's only noon for them and they have more hours in the day to accomplish some of the tasks I'm running behind on. Using time zones strategically can give you an advantage throughout the workday and week.

Cultural time zones really show how time isn't linear. If you can learn to cross from your own cultural concepts of time into another culture's, you'll become a master at time bending. We've all heard those stereotypes like "island time," "Irish time" and a "New York minute." From one culture to the next, one country or state to the next, folks handle time differently.

Now I'm generalizing here, but I speak from experience. My wife and I are both Southern and grew up in the same area of North Carolina. We went to the same high school, but because I'm Black and she's white, our communities handle time very differently—there's CPT (Colored People's Time—an outdated way of describing our laid-back approach to time) and WPT (White People's Time—an old way to refer to a more buttoned-up approach to time). But over the years, Katie and I managed to master *both* cultural time zones to our advantage. It's our superpower.

Let's say we're invited to Sunday lunch at my Memaw's church *and* to lunch at Katie's family's church. Attending both is impossible, right? How could we have lunch in two places at the same time? Easy.

In Katie's cultural time zone, church service starts early, lasts one hour and ends promptly at 11:30. By 11:40, we're eating. The dishes are in the sink at 12:30 followed by a brisk and efficient fellowship. Now over at my Memaw's church, the service ends when the preacher decides it ends. That could mean 2 pm or 3 pm. Then we fellowship, eat and we don't finish until sundown. That's two church services and lunches on the same day, a short drive away from each other. Both sides of the family are happy, our hearts are full and our stomachs are stuffed with free and delicious food.

Knowing how to cross all those different time zones, whether it's the past, present, future, East Coast or West Coast time, you can expand to CEO Life as a leader. The more open and understanding you are to respecting and transcending the zones, the more advantages you will have.

## EVERYONE GETS THE SAME 24 HOURS—WHAT ARE YOU GOING TO DO WITH YOURS?

Mid-level leaders constantly struggle with time mastery. The typical complaint you hear at this stage of growth is, "I don't have enough time!" That was me when my business first started to grow. I was scaling up, we'd just had our son, my daughter was in kindergarten, my wife was struggling and there weren't enough hours in the day.

But here's the secret about time: you and I have the same amount of time that Oprah and Bill Gates have. They built their empires with the same number of hours in the day, the week, the month and the year. But I've learned that what's more important is the value you can get out of your time. If there are 24 hours in every day, how are you going to spend them?

You have to organize your 24 hours to accommodate your *entire life.* Work is included in the waking hours, but those hours are not exclusively for work. The last thing you should do is overload your schedule with meetings. Some of your time can be dedicated to preparation and skill-building, which can help you to get more out of an hour—and you also need time for mental breaks. Exercise. Meditation. Family time. Lunch. Coffee.

Here are some examples. When you finish a call, look back over your meeting notes and look for ways you can trim some time off the next call. What time of day was your meeting? Did you have time to prepare before the call? Think of the difference it would have made to go into your meeting with an agenda, talking points, an outline and questions. The 10 minutes it takes you to get organized can shave 20 minutes off an otherwise hour-long call. Now you can take a walk!

Get effective on how long it takes to deliver a presentation or run a meeting. If you have a marketing meeting every Wednesday, you know how they go—what topic can be removed from that call to make it more efficient?

## EARLY IS ON TIME, ON TIME IS LATE

I was never an "on-time" kind of person. I was a late person. I had to work hard to be punctual, only to find out that on time is actually late. If I want to really be punctual, I have to be early—that way, I have time to get ready. Being late is disrespecting other people's time—you're telling them their schedule doesn't matter to you, and that you don't value time—theirs or yours. To be extraordinary, you can't be late.

On time is late. It is *impossible* to be a collaborative leader if you routinely deliver on time. On-time delivery leaves no time for input or feedback. If something is due at noon on Tuesday, deliver it at 9 am. That gives the recipient three hours to review it before the deadline. If the external deadline is Wednesday, meaning that's the last possible minute you can deliver the goods, then the internal deadline is Monday. No project is ever final until everyone has had the chance to collaborate, give feedback or ask questions.

One general rule on deliverables is that 48 hours should be provided to allow for everyone's true engagement. Even if you are the head of the company, telling someone you need something "by tomorrow" isn't respecting their time, work flow or the spirit of collaboration. Giving someone 48 hours is allowing them enough time to do their best. And you'll be surprised: if you give someone more time than they need, they'll typically finish it early.

## TIME IS MORE PRECIOUS THAN MONEY—MONEY CAN BE REPLENISHED WHILE TIME CANNOT

In sports, nearly everything is timed. There is nothing more exciting than a winning three-point shot right at the buzzer.

Without that last second, the result would have been very different for both teams and all the players. That last second can make or break a career.

If you're watching a scrimmage game, there's no clock and the score isn't kept. That's not the same as a game with two halves, 20 minutes each. The stakes are higher.

Business is no different. Time is a critical part of metrics and analytics in business: we look at results from month to month, quarter to quarter and year on year. What if we're talking about profits? If I say, "We made a million dollars in profits," it's very different from "We made a million dollars in profits last year," which is very different from "We made a million dollars in profits last month," which is very different from "We made a million dollars overnight." Time matters.

*"A man who dares to waste one hour of life has not discovered the value of life."*
—Charles Darwin

We can't make more time; it's a precious and limited resource. To CEO Life, you have to examine your relationship with time and money. It's perfectly fine to take time off and do nothing, but it's not okay to waste time. Doing nothing can be the most productive time you have. Some of the best ideas pop into my brain when I'm a passenger in the back of a cab or an Uber. I wasn't "doing anything," but that time just became valuable. On the other hand, you're probably not going to generate a bunch of creative and revolutionary ideas watching five seasons of a reality dating show. That's time you can't get back, and it reinforces the mistaken belief that time isn't valuable.

## CRISIS MANAGEMENT WASTES TIME AND ENERGY

In racing, pit crews accomplish their precision tasks in seconds. For many, the pressure would be intolerable. However, for these highly-trained teams, standards are set; roles are clear; tasks are outlined; the process is sequenced and their transition is timed. The pit crew is dealing with crisis management and they're prepared for it. They are trained and have highly specialized skills. They also use their telescopic focus to try to avoid a crisis —that way, they just have to do maintenance during the race when it counts. They're proactive instead of reactive. That's why they're so effective.

Being proactive means preparing. When you're not prepared, you waste energy and time. Time is the same when you're in a crisis as when you're preparing, but it's easy to waste time during a crisis because you're putting out fires instead of moving forward. Twenty minutes of preparation can save you from all those little fires so you don't lose momentum and you continue to progress.

In February 2020, I had just completed a leader-training retreat with Primo managers. We had decided that the future and growth of our company depended upon the strength and readiness of our management team. A few weeks later, the pandemic hit. Talk about a crisis! The food service industry was about to take a major hit like never before.

But we had such a solid team of leaders in place, we were able to pivot our focus. Instead of looking at how we could increase sales at our franchises, we focused on how we could *further* prepare and cultivate our team. The tumultuous years of 2020 and 2021 ended up being a period of unprecedented growth for Primo. Our pit crew was ready for anything, and when a crisis hit, we didn't lose momentum, finishing way ahead of our goal.

## YOUR BODY CLOCK GIVES YOU CLUES

We all have our own "internal clock." That means that each of us marches to our own internal rhythm. Depending on our chemical and biological make-up, some of us are early risers and some of us are night owls. Some of us need a solid 10 hours of sleep for our bodies and brains to recover from our day, while others only need four. Some of us can fall asleep anywhere, anytime. Some of us need black-out shades, Bluetooth headphone sleep masks with guided sleep meditation and CBD sleep aids to fall asleep. Some of us wake up seven times a night, and some of us sleep straight through. Regardless of how often or long you sleep, it's important to *know yourself.*

In addition to knowing how much and what kind of rest and recovery you need, it's important that you know when you're at your best. If you're an early riser, you might finish a five-mile run and do your best and clearest thinking before 8 am. But if you're someone who stays up until 2 am, you may sleep in until 10, have a leisurely morning and schedule all your hardest work for late afternoon. There's no right or wrong way to go about your day; it's only important that you *know yourself.*

In addition to knowing yourself, you also have to know and respect your co-workers and colleagues: they may operate totally differently than you. Maybe someone has a new baby, and even though she used to be ready to jump on a call at 6 am, she's now waking up every two hours for feedings and her life is turned upside down. It's your job to know and respect that. Maybe your co-worker is a family man and has to pick up his kids from school, so everything in his work day has to happen before 2 pm. Know and respect that.

Pay attention to when your own brain and spirit are most energized to accomplish a set of tasks or functions and perform your highest-value work. Once you know yourself and your co-workers, you will know the best way to organize your day, week and month ahead.

As you plan out your day and week, keep your own personal body clock in mind. Just like an athlete, if you are someone who works in sprints, then you have to spend time recovering to replenish your energy and oxygen. In addition to your meetings, calls and administrative work, here is a short list of valuable tasks you need to regularly budget into your schedule:

1. **Deep Thinking**: You may want to schedule this for mid-week once you've had a few work days with new information coming in. By centering yourself in the middle of the week to focus on the present moment, you can do that time-bending we talked about, and incorporate events from the recent past (what happened on Monday) so you can visualize the immediate future (the goals you want to reach by Friday).
2. **Strategizing:** Your strategy focus is the telescopic view of your goals for this week, this month, this quarter, this year and 10 years from now.
3. **Brainstorming:** Some people brainstorm with a pen and paper, writing out their thoughts freestyle. Some people need to be "doing nothing": driving, taking a shower or other rote activities, and they record their thoughts as they come up. Whatever works for you, be sure to budget in time for this kaleidoscopic focus.
4. **Deep-drill Tactical Execution:** This is when you're using that microscopic view on a specific problem or goal. Know how you do this best: do you need total seclusion without any distraction? Do you need white noise? Your laptop or a pen and paper? Know yourself, and schedule time during the day and week for this intense focus.
5. **Analyzing Data:** Unless you allow time for analysis, whether it's staffing or a budget, you need to set aside specific time to review all the information that is coming at you. This preparation allows you to go into every meeting informed, focused and ready.
6. **Assessment and Evaluation:** Maybe a good time to schedule this task is at the end of the week. You can

> look back at your accomplishments and review the stretches and strengths. What could you have done better? What did you do better than you expected? If you reached an important goal this week, what helped you achieve it? What would you do differently next time?

If you don't plan ahead to include these tasks, your day will turn into chaos and you'll burn out quickly. Speaking of burning out, you also have to schedule in free time. Dan Sullivan, strategic coach and author of *Who Not How,* talks about how you can achieve more by doing less. He schedules 155 free days at the beginning of every year, and 210 work days.

Many entrepreneurs think that you have to work every day to succeed, but by working for yourself, you're trying to achieve the freedom to work how you want and when you want. That means you have to schedule in that freedom from the very beginning of your business. You will find that you achieve more on those 210 work days than you would if you worked 365. To be a high performer, your workflow requires both focus and recovery. Recover on your free days, and on your work days, you'll be immersed in high-quality, focused attention—which leads to quality results.

When I was in college, I managed my time in chunks. I built my week with blocks of time on the calendar, each block dedicated to a specific activity. Tuesday and Thursday were my heavy class days, and today those remain my heavy, public-facing meeting days. I intentionally scheduled no classes on Mondays and Fridays, making those days available for work or a free day. Wednesdays were for homework, and today I reserve them for special projects that are not part of my daily work flow. If Tuesday is an intense day, then homework—or presentation preparation—needs to be done on Wednesday before class or calls on Thursday. I also try not to have meetings before 10:30 am so there's time in the morning for my important self-care routines, like meditation and exercise.

## THE MORE WE VALUE OUR LIVES, THE MORE WE PAY ATTENTION TO HOW WE USE TIME

Workaholics live shorter, less productive and less happy lives. We hear a lot about work-life balance these days. But what is "life?" Aside from "work," most successful CEOs have many components that make up their lives: family, health, sports, art, faith, hobbies, self-care and education or learning. These things combined with work make up their whole life, and they have to find a way to balance all of them to be wholly successful.

If you think of balancing your life on a scale, you'd have work on one side and everything else on the other. But this isn't an effective way of managing your life or your time. It's not work versus life; it's all connected. Your physical, mental and emotional health, family, relationships and work are not separate points on a line, they are all the valuable aspects of your life. They are arranged in a circle, not on opposite sides of a scale.

I like Tony Robbins's Wheel of Life model. He asks that you look at each area of value in your life as a spoke on a wheel: when they are all given different levels of attention, they can't form a circle, and consequently the wheel is thrown off balance. When you take a higher (or telescopic) view of each area of your life, you can determine where you are succeeding, excelling, growing and where you need to improve. What area needs more focus? You can revisit this model every few years as your priorities and life circumstances change. For instance, if you're in your 20s, single and without kids, you can put a little more attention on developing and cultivating professional relationships. But if you're married with a house full of kids with sports and school activities, you'll be thinking differently!

Another tool Robbins uses is the Pyramid of Mastery, which is a map for prioritizing each area of your life. At the base of the pyramid is your physical health—without that, you cannot achieve anything in life. Next are your emotions, then your relationships, time, career and life mission, followed by finances, with your contribution and spirit at the top. You can't achieve the ultimate and most important aspects of life—your spirit and contributions to this world—without a solid foundation of everything else.

## THE THREE MYTHS ABOUT TIME

When you're a business owner and entrepreneur, you are in charge of your time. This can feel overwhelming, especially if you wear a lot of hats and haven't yet learned to delegate. You can get so focused on developing your business that it's easy to lose sight of your whole-life priorities. You also may have been taught some old-school thinking about how to spend your time, or maybe you just need to hit refresh and get a new perspective.

Somewhere along the way, you probably developed the belief that the more time you spend on your business, the more successful you'll be as a CEO. It's just not that simple. We already talked about the importance of budgeting in free days, and how you have to move away from the idea that constantly grinding is going to give you the results you want. There are a number of long-held misconceptions about the relationship between time and business success that need to be challenged and rejected. As you really focus in on how you spend your time—your most valuable resource—keep the following three myths in mind:

### I. Multitasking is Good Time Management

All the studies and literature on productivity and brain function have debunked this myth. While we may be able to do many things at once, human beings are not wired to do several disparate things *well* at the same time. Study after study has revealed that when we multitask, we make more mistakes, our memory and ability to retain information are impaired, our problem-solving ability declines and we can even become depressed. The bottom line is that our brains just don't have the cognitive building blocks to properly focus on more than one task at a time. Multitasking puts too many demands on our brains.

Focusing intently on one task at a time allows us to do quality work, and it's the best use of our time. When we have clear priorities, goals and deadlines, we can harness our powerful, microscopic focus. If we go one step further and eliminate distractions like noise, TV, interruptions, meetings or alerts from our phone, we can achieve deep focus and flow—which then allows us to deliver a higher-quality result.

**II. More Time Creates Better Results**

A 30-minute meeting can be infinitely more efficient than a one or three-hour meeting. When the duration is shortened, participants are less distracted and more committed to achieving the meeting's goal within that time frame. Also, meetings should start and end on time. If you know you only have 20 minutes to deliver information, you will be more likely to go into the meeting prepared with concise and well-focused talking points, therefore delivering better results. Blocking out three hours for a call allows for a lot of side conversations, topic tangents, distractions and interruptions. Your ability to focus and prioritize is directly related to your efficiency, and the more you master those skills, the better and faster your results will be.

**III. A CEO's Time Is More Important than Anyone Else's Time**

Everyone's time is important. How a CEO uses their employees' time is revealing of organizational culture and workplace satisfaction. Employee surveys regularly give higher marks to the CEO who provides quality time on a consistent basis rather than only appearing when there is a problem.

As a CEO, if you are communicating the message that "my time is more important than yours" simply because of your title or status, you are creating a toxic environment where workers feel unvalued. Everyone has 24 hours in the day, and those hours are created equal—they are not replenishable or replaceable for anyone. Abusing other people's time cultivates bitterness and resentment. Respecting everyone's time equally shows that you know every single person is contributing an important role to the success of the company. Allow yourself to be present, available and respectful—to the janitor as well as to the CFO.

## MANAGE PRIORITIES TO MASTER TIME

Instead of concentrating on managing your available time, think of it as managing your daily priorities. Most people monitor two things in their lives: their calendar and their checkbook. Almost everything they value can be found there. But what if instead, you arranged your actions around a list of priorities for the day?

*"Time management requires self-discipline, self-mastery and self-control more than anything else."*
—Brian Tracy

Block out your time around people. In looking at the day, week, month and year ahead, think in terms of "daughter time," "family time," "vacation time" and "self-care time." Then you can block out "activity time," which is business-related. But even those time blocks are people-oriented. A meeting with your CFO is an opportunity to connect with the person running the finances of your organization, and he or she deserves your presence and mindful attention.

A meeting with your marketing team prioritizes the people who do the hard work to help your company connect with the community and other businesses. By thinking of your time in terms of people, you are choosing to center those you value the most and communicating that priority to others. Once you've made time for the people in your life, everything else is an activity on your to-do list.

The resulting success will be a reflection of your choices, and ultimately it's your choices that determine your destiny—not chance.

## THERE'S FORTUNE IN THE FOLLOW THROUGH

Here's a quick cheat sheet that will help you transition from "time management" to "priority management." You can follow these steps when blocking out your day, week, month, quarter and year.

1. People first, activities second. Always block out the priorities around people first. Update your one, seven and 30-day calendar to reflect this shift in priorities.
2. Write down your activities as a to-do list. Now prioritize each of these tasks. What are the top three? Keep in mind that there will never be enough time to complete everything. Accept that as a fact of life. You can't do everything.
3. Accomplish task number one and don't move on to number two until number one is complete.
    - If you are interrupted, go back to number one until it is complete.
    - Delegate. If you're overloaded and someone else can do it, don't.
    - Repeat this system for all your schedules and calendars, from your daily agenda to your long-term annual plan.

Break it down
Mission
Goal
Project
Task
@Quoted Visually

# CHAPTER 9
# SELF•ISH$^2$
## RECHARGING BY RETREATING

*"Come with me by yourselves to a quiet place and get some rest."*
—Jesus (Mark 6:31)

You are a battery: a walking, talking vessel of energy that you dispense throughout the day, into your career, parenting, partnership journey and your life. But batteries require charging or changing. A dead battery is no use to anyone. And in order to be a charged-up, operating-at-full-capacity, self-aware self•*ish* servant, you need to know how to fill yourself with the right kind of operating fuel.

Just as when you leave the lights on in the car, there are a lot of things that drain your battery: unhealthy relationships that have run their course, a sudden attack on the health of a close family member or even a few consecutive nights of bad sleep. Tossing and turning or ruminating about a problem can deplete your energy and capacity to get through the day.

But to be a high-caliber self•*ish* servant, you have to keep yourself charged. Back in Chapter 2, I taught you about the importance of being *self-ish,* and how by investing in yourself, you're putting on your oxygen mask—a requirement before you can help someone else. Just like you can't assist others when you yourself can't breathe, you can't feed and nourish a family, team or company when your energy is drained and you're operating on nothing. And to do any of this successfully, you need keen self-awareness.

There are lots of ways to recharge, and you can even upgrade your power capacity in big and small ways. I've learned over the years that in addition to recharging, every new phase of life also requires a reboot: a conscious commitment to introspection and growth, and an honest accounting of the self-limiting behaviors that are holding you back from reaching your potential.

The great thing about potential is that it grows as you grow. With every new lesson you learn, challenge you face and goal you accomplish, you're expanding your potential. It's like your inner vessel has grown and you need to learn new ways to fill it. Upgrading your charge capacity is upgrading your potential, allowing you to reach new heights and bigger, bolder, more audacious goals.

So, how do you recharge, reboot and reset? The first thing you need to do is make a commitment: vow to always invest in yourself so that you can invest in others. You can do a big reset once a year, a weekly reset every Sunday and a daily reset with self-care practices. I do all of these, and as a result, I've been inspired to invest in my team. Primo sends its executive team on wellness retreats for leadership and mentoring every year.

Because I acknowledge that these transformational experiences have made me into the man and leader that I am, who lives the CEO Life every day, I want to provide the same service to the people I mentor. That way, they will feel valued and develop meaningful self-care practices, then go on to become servant leaders who develop their teams in the same way: it's the circle of self!

## BIG, ANNUAL SYSTEM UPGRADE

My Outward Bound experience challenged everything I thought I knew about life, the world and myself. The lessons I learned in those 30 days provided a system upgrade that shaped me so dramatically, it stays with me to this day. My belief in myself, my abilities and my potential was expanded at a pivotal time in my life, and that sustained me for years.

As I grew older and my business empire expanded to multiple locations, I began operating multiple brands in different sectors—franchising, real estate and coaching. Meanwhile, my family had grown: I had two kids, a wife and a lot on my plate. I started feeling like my leadership skills were outdated. Just like all the devices we use require regular upgrades to keep them functioning and improve their performance, I felt the need to hone and expand my capacity and potential.

My wife Katie and I love to travel—it's truly one of the most valuable gifts of CEO Life. We make our travel purposeful and categorize our travel into one of several "buckets." Each of these categories fulfills something different: Do we need to reset our relationship? Do we need to escape our hectic lives? Do we need new challenges to build our self-confidence?

Bucket one is the R&R reset. This means luxury all the way: being spoiled with first-class hospitality and hours on end at the beach. The biggest decision we make is when to start drinking cocktails with umbrellas and when to switch from the sand and crystal-clear sea to a poolside cabana. This type of self-care is an escape from routine, requirements and real life stresses.

Travel bucket number two is the exploration and experience reboot. This is an adventure that expands our minds and knowledge about the world. We might paraglide over the Caribbean, zip-line through the jungles of Costa Rica or museum-hop through the winding streets of Paris. Our days are packed with stimulating, sensory experiences that invigorate and expand us in new, meaningful and powerful ways.

The third travel bucket that has served us is the "go and become" adventure. This is a trip that prompts and fosters growth. It's an opportunity to elevate our partnership and relationship, and invigorate how we show up for each other, our family and our community. This trip really focuses on putting the self•*ish* in travel: self-reflection, self-exploration and self-love. There are three- to four-day trips we can take nearby to fulfill this travel need (we like the Art of Living Retreat Center, which is a short drive from our home). Those trips aren't big on luxury, but they're transformative.

The most impactful "go and become" trip we've experienced is in Tecate, Mexico, and it combines *all three* travel styles in one: luxury, experience and self-expansion. The Rancho La Puerta resort is a yearly destination for Katie and me, as well as for the Primo executive team.

Like the Outward Bound experience, a trip to Rancho La Puerta changes and challenges me mentally, emotionally and spiritually. Instead of roughing it on a backwoods trail with a backpack and dried fruit and nuts for breakfast, lunch and dinner, we enjoy clean, beautiful accommodations and gourmet, nourishing meals that focus on health and clean eating. Like the mountains of Montana, we're off the grid and unplugged—but it's different because we're sitting in a comfortable room in front of a fireplace.

Rancho La Puerta challenges visitors to go outside their comfort zone with daily activities that make them push their boundaries: yoga, sound healing, salsa dancing, chocolate and wine pairing classes, mindfulness meditation and chanting. The instructors are from all over the world and are committed to each visitor's overall well-being. In the evening, we read, journal or dine with wine at La Cocina Que Canta ("The Kitchen that Sings"). Rancho La Puerta is a whole life experience.

Yearly trips to reboot your life don't have to be extravagant. You can challenge yourself to hike further than ever and explore the Appalachian Trail. You can spend five days in a national park, sleeping in a tent listening to the coyotes. You can sign up for a cooking class in New York City or a silent meditation retreat in Massachusetts or Santa Barbara. Commit to giving yourself a yearly reset that expands your capacity and recharges you for the year to come. This commitment is a vital and invaluable way to become a high-caliber leader, and the *only* way to become a truly self•*ish* servant leader.

## WEEKLY, MONTHLY AND QUARTERLY REBOOTS

I like to take a quarterly look at my life. Every 90 days, I give myself a mini three-day weekend off, and sometimes I push it to five. I review my life balance so that I am integrating change regularly. I step out of my routine so I can refuel and prepare for the quarter ahead feeling refreshed and energized.

During one of these quarterly breaks, I decided to review my mental fitness, following the suggestions of Shirzad Chamine. This self-reflection led me to meet my inner judge and master saboteur—that little voice in my head that obsesses about my mistakes and failures, worries compulsively and obsesses about the future. That inner judge condemns me, my circumstances and my choices as well as those of other people, magnifying my insecurities by allowing my ego to take over, ranking people in order of their worth. What are the parts of my mind that operate on negative emotions like fear, doubt and anxiety? How does that thinking impact my work, self-confidence and relationships?

I already knew that I was a hyper-achiever from a very young age. That's great, right? I'm always setting the bar higher and higher for myself so that I'm outranking even my highest standards. Wrong. This is one of my inner saboteurs. Being a hyper-achiever is fear-based. It's rooted in feeling powerless, and comes from my childhood with a mom who was struggling. I was powerless to help her and fix things. I had a deeply-ingrained fear that created my hyper-achieving drive, and it has had a negative impact on my life and my relationships. Before I came to this realization, I had gotten into the habit of prioritizing my achievements and accomplishments over the people in my life, and over my own personal health. There were times when I would go *months* with no more than four hours of sleep each night, which had a detrimental impact on my weight and heart health. Using Shirzad Chamine's Saboteur Assessment (positiveintelligence.com/saboteurs), I learned that to overcome those ingrained behaviors that sabotage me, I could focus my awareness on the "sage" region of my brain. I asked myself new questions, and remained curious and open to new answers:

1. How can I be creative and innovative with how I use my time?
2. How can I reshape my work life so that the outcome is still satisfying and I feel pride, but not to the detriment of my health and relationships?
3. How can I stop trying to control the outcome of things beyond my control?

The answers to these questions have changed how I operate daily. I prioritize every goal and event by the day, week, month and quarter. I improve my communication with my inner circle so that everyone is on the same page. I give myself two minutes every day, three times a day to do something that enriches my intelligence in a positive way. These changes have pulled me out of unconscious, self-detrimental behaviors and have given me clarity and serenity. There are other ways to reboot every few months using tools that help you visualize and take action toward your goals. Vision-boarding, action-boarding, journaling, day-long seminars and guided meditation classes are all great techniques to refresh and recharge.

*"Write the vision and make it plain on tablets, that he may run who reads it."*

—Habakkuk 2:2-3

## DAILY RECHARGE

You have to invest in yourself every day. Recharging requires daily maintenance and minute-to-minute choices that can shape your performance and experience. I think the most valuable technique to improve your daily outlook is to add a new event to your schedule: something to look forward to.

Studies have shown that being excited about a future event improves your mood, reduces stress, increases motivation, stimulates creativity and energizes you as you work toward your goals. The anticipation of that future event can trigger the release of feel-good neurotransmitters, like dopamine, oxytocin and endorphins. Whether it's a concert, a trip or a night out with friends, schedule something fun and organize your work life around it.

Other studies show that while cardio is a big part of heart and mental health, it's also important to stand instead of sit for hours on end. Standing while you work can shed 88 calories each hour, and means less back and neck pain, better blood circulation and a faster metabolism. Some people take this philosophy even further and focus on their core muscles while they stand, or install a treadmill under their desk so they can get their steps in while they type. I think it's a great way to bring awareness to your physical and mental health, even passively.

Other important daily reboots include breaks. Schedule time for a mental break each day that pulls you out of your behavior and routines. Take a walk outside without headphones so you're getting fresh air and visual stimulation. Sit in a dog park and watch the little guys' joy at being off-leash. Schedule a lunch date with a friend or partner. Surprise your wife with flowers. Plan a movie outing with your kids. Read a book for 30 minutes. Listen to music. Meditate. Pray. Seek teachings and connection with yourself and others. Fill your inner vessel and recharge your battery so you are fulfilled and available to be of service for others—a successful, self•*ish* servant.

## THERE'S FORTUNE IN THE FOLLOW THROUGH

1. List the top seven words that describe you with a full battery, then list their opposites. Which of these show up when your battery is drained?
2. Where is your biggest opportunity for staying supercharged? Focus on your daily and weekly routines, monthly and quarterly reboots or on big annual upgrades. Which represents the supercharger?
3. There's power in focusing on one word to constantly align your energy and effort for an extended period of time. It could be one of your seven full battery words from above, or an entirely new skill that you need to develop. For the next year, what is the *one word* that you will affirm, learn more about and grow into as part of your CEO identity?

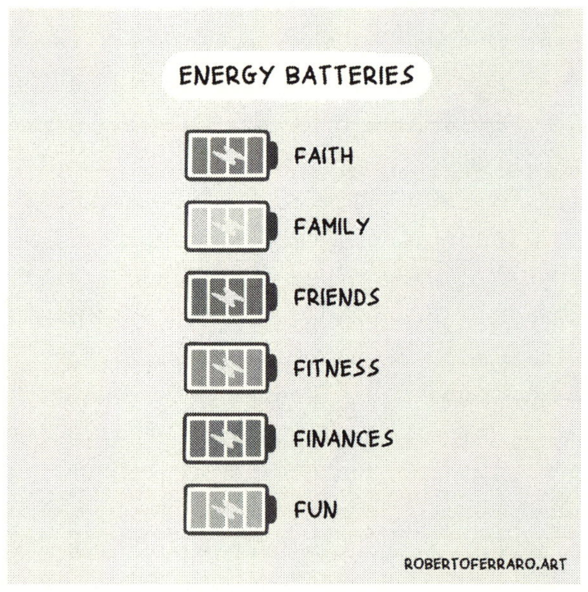

# CHAPTER 10
# GRATITUDE + SERVICE
## APPRECIATE LIKE MEMAW

*"I count my blessings, and I'm so blessed. [It's] very easy. I could spend all day and all night counting millions of blessings. I've been very blessed."*
—Deborah Szekely, 102-year-old owner of Rancho La Puerta

Memaw spoke all of the love languages fluently. It might be hard to believe that a Black woman born in Goldston, North Carolina in 1936 could be a master of communication in five languages, but Memaw was such a servant that she wanted everyone she met to feel loved. Knowing their language meant she could love them just right.

She was named Arzelia Headen at birth, but when she was a teenager, she took on the nickname Zate. She was known for her beauty, inside and out. She helped to raise her siblings, nieces and nephews before raising her own two kids, and then she helped to raise me. Just by being herself and loving people as much as she did, she became fluent in the five love languages.

In his book *The 5 Love Languages,* Gary Chapman outlines a clear way to give and receive love in every type of relationship by learning how to communicate effectively in ways that center other people's needs. Learning to speak another person's love language is the ultimate form of service. Memaw never read Chapman's book, but she didn't have to.

According to Chapman, the five categories describe how people interpret "love" based on how others speak or behave around them. The five languages are: words of affirmation, quality time, physical touch, acts of service and receiving gifts. Most people are strongly one or the other with a close second. In relationships—whether it's a romantic partner, a friend, a colleague or an acquaintance, it's the ultimate sign of respect to understand how others feel appreciated, centered, seen and loved. So to be a true servant, it is more important to learn another person's love language than to know your own.

Your boyfriend presents you with a bag of sunflower seeds because he knows it makes you think of when you were a kid and your dad took you to baseball games. If your love language is receiving gifts, you light up and tears come to your eyes. You feel appreciated because you know he listens to you, and you feel loved because it means he was thinking of you when he was going about his day.

Maybe you're a mom who is always running around taking your kids to sports practice, preparing their meals, cleaning up their messes and doing everyone's laundry. Your partner presents you with a card that says, "We couldn't do any of this without you, thank you for being the glue that holds our family together." Your kids thank you and tell you they love you every morning on their way out the door. If your love language is words of affirmation, then you have no problem continuing to be of service—you feel seen and appreciated because you're getting and feeling the love you need.

Your mom lives alone, and even though she spends her time doing things she loves like gardening and going to church functions, you know that if you plan a weekly trip to the mall followed by a sit-down lunch, she'll feel remembered and special. Her love language is quality time, and feeling like she can connect with you, be a part of your life and tell you how her tomato plants are doing makes her feel loved.

Your husband has a bad back from an ancient sports injury, and by the end of the week, it flares up from stress. On Saturday morning, you bring him coffee when he wakes up, an ice pack and two ibuprofen. Then he hears the lawn mower out front because you paid the neighbor kid to cut the grass so he can rest. You took the liberty of scheduling an afternoon appointment with the chiropractor so he doesn't have to start the week in pain. He immediately feels the stress leave his body and he feels cherished. You know that his love language is acts of service.

Your best friend is going through a bad divorce. You check in with her every day, and ask her if there's anything you can do to help. She says she's got it and doesn't need anything, but you know she's lonely. You show up at her doorstep on your way home from work just to give her a hug and present her with a gift certificate for a massage. You've known her a long time, and you know that her love language is physical touch, which she's been lacking through this whole process. That hug and the massage will get her brain to release oxytocin, which will help her feel happier, reduce stress and give her a dose of the love that has been missing.

Memaw spoke all five love languages to me and other people, but the first thing she did was make sure you had a full belly. No matter how little money was coming in, she always had food on the stove for anyone who walked through the door. (In a way, this ruined me: I became so accustomed to someone else making me a plate and cleaning up after me that I never really learned to do those things for myself.) She turned a pot of fried potatoes and onions into a pot of gold as an act of service to our neighborhood.

Memaw made people feel special because she made sure time spent with her was quality time. She was everyone's favorite drinking partner—including mine—and going round-for-round with her gave you time to empty your heart and mind of all that ailed you. She believed that a beer was the best bounce-back from life's worst problems, and having one together made people feel special. Even just sitting on her couch watching *Wheel of Fortune, Jeopardy* or *The Young and the Restless* was quality time.

No one could give you a cussing out like Memaw. If you crossed her, you'd be on the receiving end of a passionate verbal lashing that would make the devil blush. But the opposite was also true: no one could hug you up with physical affection and make you feel like a million bucks better than Memaw. She was a crafty storyteller and could hold an audience in the retelling of her favorite memories. When I was growing up, I would hear her bragging to other people about how I could count to 1,000 by the time I was three. Whenever company was visiting, I'd start counting and I'd still be going long after they left. She made me feel special and confident.

Gifts from her were all the more special because she had limited means. My whole life, she gave me loving cards on my birthday or on holidays with five dollars tucked inside, or just a brown bag with some nuts, apples or raisins.

I talk to my family frequently about the five love languages. Memaw spoke those languages intuitively, but I really put in the effort to know the primary and secondary love languages of the dozen or so people closest to me. Learning my daughter Nia's love language was a real learning curve. She doesn't care about tangible gifts—maybe because she grew up with most of the things she wants and needs. Her primary love language is acts of service, and her secondary is words of affirmation. Any time she has a major success—she's added to the honor roll, makes a great play in sports or gets inducted into the National Junior Honor Society (yes, I'm bragging), she feels loved when I tell her how proud I am of her. She doesn't need me to slip her a few extra dollars or take her shopping. I tell her, "I love you" and "I'm proud of you" and I give her compliments.

## WORKPLACE GRATITUDE AND APPRECIATION

My mother-in-law Terri's best friend is Dottie. Dottie is the owner of Southern Supreme Fruitcake Kitchen, and I get to express my gratitude to her *and* hundreds of my colleagues by creating a yearly "fruitcake list." I kill two birds with one stone by supporting a local, family-owned business and sending golden fruitcakes to hundreds of people each year. This has become the signature Primo gift, and I always include a personal thank-you note.

As a business owner and entrepreneur, I've noticed that there's an appreciation deficit in the professional world. I want Primo to live up to its core value of World-Class Hospitality, and we can't do that unless we live it and teach it. We've created an Appreciation at Work Training Tool, which we incorporate into the first 90 days of employment at the Primo Kulture Lab—a training program that teaches new hires about our values, company ethos and performance expectations.

Once a staff member is integrated into their team, they learn each person's primary and secondary love language, and teach theirs to their colleagues. We also talk about each person's "irrelevant love language," the one that doesn't really matter much to them. We have translated this philosophy into a workplace training module that we call the Five Appreciation Languages, teaching our teams how to express appreciation and read the cues that others need to feel appreciated. We also cover appropriate workplace displays of appreciation (for example, a high-five instead of a slap on the butt like in sports).

We model and teach gratitude as a life practice to members of our organization with regular expressions of our gratitude, and by encouraging staff to mirror our examples. I am a servant to my staff, who in turn are servants to their co-workers and customers.

**Daily**

- We invite our staff to practice the SAVERS routine: Silence, Affirmations, Visualization, Exercise, Reading and Scribing (see Chapter 4 for more details).
- We ask our team to think of three things each day that they appreciate. These things can be as simple as the weather or the music of birds chirping. Or they can be something profound, like loving relationships, a big occasion or an accomplishment.
- We distribute High Performance Planners created by Brendan Burchard to advanced leaders in our organization to support their thoughtful appreciation of others.
- Personally, I start and finish every day with gratitude. First thing in the morning, I take in some fresh air, face the sun and activate my brain. Next, I write down three appreciations in my journal. At the end of every day, I write down three more things I'm grateful for plus three wins or "amazements" from the day. I pick a person every day to appreciate—well, I started with one, then added another and another—I'm up to five people each day who I thank, whether it's through a phone call, an email, a text or a gesture.

**Weekly**

- We begin meetings by expressing our personal and professional "bests" of the week.
- At each meeting, we share "brag headlines," recognizing members of our organization who are standing out.
- Everyone is responsible for bringing in quality updates on their own weekly highlights, and giving

shout-outs to other team members, co-workers and staff.
- We have a weekly "hospitality recognition" winner.
- We have a weekly Primo Service Rockstar, for someone who exemplifies our values in their daily performance.

**Monthly**

- Each month, we have a team newsletter where we call out our Hospitality All-Stars.
- We celebrate every staff member's birthday, promotion or important anniversary.
- Every quarter, we immerse our staff in the highest-end category of service—coffee shops, five-star restaurants and the best quick-service restaurants.

**Annually**

- We have fun, light-hearted competitions each year. Leaders strive to win the Primo Way Award, the Primo Worldwide Award and the Numbers Don't Lie Award.
- There is a yearly award for the Primo All-Star Team.
- To the partner who has continuously exemplified platinum-level servant leadership, we award the coveted Service Mastery Award. All of these awards are given out in person at our annual team gathering.

## FOR MEMAW

When I was in high school, I wrote a book of appreciation for Memaw and my mom called *Two Angelic Creations*. I'm sharing the introduction below in the hopes that I'll inspire you to express your gratitude for the people you love.

---

*This book is written to recap the lives of my Grandmother, Arzelia, and Mother, Myron. Both of them have lived very interesting lives. Lives of struggle, perseverance and growth. I am so grateful that they are here for me. Without them, I would not be. With them, I have everything I need. They are my two Guardian Angels. I am so lucky. Sorry rest of the world, but they are ALL mine. My Memaw tries so hard to baby me, and my Mommy's goal is to make me a man. Memaw tucks me in every night, while Mommy makes me buy my own cover. They are so unique; this book is their introduction, telling where they have been and where they are going. Unfortunately for you, an introduction is about all you can get because I am VERY possessive of MY angels.*

---

When Memaw died in 2017, I memorialized her with the poem below.

> ***A**uthentic*
> ***R**espectful*
> ***Z**esty*
> ***E**asy going*
> ***L**aid back*
> ***I**nspiring*
> *ALWAYS LOVED*
> *Memaw Zate da Kata*
> *There's no place I'd rather be; Than 3.2.4. Tuff Street*
> *This is where it all began; For me & the rest of the Headen Klan*
> *There's always some pots on the stove, and up and down the road, everybody just…floats*
> *Inside 324 is a Queen on her throne*
> *Call her Arzelia, Zate, Memaw…just BET not say it wrong*

*Ring-Ring-Ring, UP, there's the telephone*
*Better not be 'bout no gutters…"Oh hey Bessie, I love you too.*
*My story Young and the Restless on, you can call me after 2."*
*I believe it's 'bout time for Larry, I know he'll be here soon.*
*And if Myron ever get out of church, we'll gone ahead & heat the food.*
*Let me see that phone again, see how cold it is outside*
*663-2121; Lord we gone freeze it's 65.*
*Go get some wood for the stove…Oh I forgot it's 2017*
*Turn up the gas and bring my "snuggie" out here with the sleeves*
*HOPE-TO-DIE, Sholl would love me some ice cream.*
*Shame, ya grandbaby sell it, ain't even none in the cabinator*
*Keep telling me to share with the family, that pint there is Zate da Katas,*
*"Anyway, Tonio bout time for Dancing with the Stars"*
*"Memaw, I believe it's 'bout time for bed, get ready for tomorrow?"*
*"Oh, I don't go no bed this early, be 'bout quarter to one"*
*"Fine, Zate da Kata, suit ya self, I'm tired, I'm done"*
*Just a day in the life of the funniest woman ever known*
*And did I mention strong…so strong no way she's ever really gone*
*An Angelic Spirit like hers can only live on*
*And on*
*And on.*

---

Being of service to others came naturally to Memaw, but above all else, she was always of humble service to God. Memaw ended every day on her knees in prayer, expressing her gratitude and thanking God for the abundance in her life. It's really trendy these days to talk about gratitude, but Memaw was ahead of her time. She lived her gratitude to God through being of service to others. She was a servant leader before there was a label for it: a prime example of living in gratitude.

I live my life in service of all that she gave me. While she was here, I always did my best for her. With my first scholarship money, I paid to have plumbing installed in her house. She slept on the same mattress my whole life, and I bought her a brand new one so she could sleep like a queen. But my most important tribute to her is living in gratitude, and expressing that gratitude to God and to others in daily, tangible ways. The biggest ingredient in the self•*ish* servant recipe is that we all need to show appreciation like Memaw. Even if your actual Memaw is no longer with you on earth, as you Create Extra•Ordinary Life, I hope you frequently ask yourself the bold questions, *"Who is my Memaw?"* I also hope you follow it up with, *"Who can I be Memaw to?"*

## THERE'S FORTUNE IN THE FOLLOW THROUGH

Memaw spoke all five love languages intuitively, but it doesn't come that easily to everyone. This is an opportunity to hone in on your own love languages and be a self•*ish* servant by learning to speak the love languages of those around you.

1. What are your primary, secondary and blindspot love languages?
2. What are the primary, secondary and blindspot love languages of your inner circle?
3. Who do you lean on for Memaw-like appreciation and

love, and who will you commit to bringing Memaw-like appreciation and love to?

# ABOUT THE AUTHOR

Antonio McBroom is the co-founder of Primo Partners as well as a professional speaker, author, coach, serial entrepreneur, social justice advocate and real estate developer. Going from ice cream scooper to Ben & Jerry's youngest franchisee and CEO of a $20M+ annual business, he passionately pursues his goal of leaving a $10B+ legacy and impact on Black business excellence. McBroom is a purposeful philanthropist who serves as an active member and international missionary leader at his church New Hope. He resides in North Carolina with his wife and two children. *The Selfish Servant* is his second book.

For more information about Antonio McBroom and additional resources for *The Self•ish Servant,* scan the QR code below:

# ABOUT THE PUBLISHER

Legacy Launch Pad is a boutique publishing company that works with entrepreneurs from all over the world. For more information about Legacy Launch Pad, go to:

www.legacylaunchpadpub.com

Made in the USA
Columbia, SC
10 March 2025